AN ALCOHOLIC'S
ANONYMOUS EX

http://www.mehab.website

AN ALCOHOLIC'S ANONYMOUS EX

ISBN-13: 978-1539706434
ISBN-10: 1539706435

Beverage illustrations within this book were created by Marco Serido, **MarcoSerido.com**.

With love and appreciation
for everything A to Z

Table of Contents

Side Work

Suggested pairing: Screaming Nazi

The drink with a name so obscenely inappropriate, it's embarrassing to even ask for but exactly what you want. Kind of like a book about someone's alcoholism with cocktail recipes included.

1 part Rumple Minze

1 part Jägermeister

Pour equal parts of both liquors in shot glass and enjoy.

Cheers.

In the spirit of AA, allow me to introduce myself. Hi, my name is Sherry, and I am an alcoholic's anonymous ex. No, I do not have a drinking problem. No, I was not in the program. No, I don't care if you think I'm an insensitive asshole for making light of a serious disease.

That being said, yes, I have experienced the ultimate universal fuck you, having survived, albeit not without scars, living through my ex-husband's alcoholism and its everlasting aftermath.

Mixing drinks with stories about addiction may seem unsympathetic and possibly offensive. I get it. But I like plays on words and I find that adult beverages facilitate having to swallow stories like these. Wine makes just about everything go down easier.

Let's do some sidework, shall we? If you've ever been a bartender then you are keenly aware that in order to prepare for long a shift behind the bar, there are certain details that must be addressed so that you don't end up in the weeds later on. Fruit needs to be cut, ice bins filled, cash counted, mixes prepared, et cetera, et cetera, et fucking cetera. It takes a little bit of time and it isn't the most thrilling experience, but it is a necessary evil.

But if, like me, you aren't much of a rule follower and you prefer to slice lemons at a later time, it's all good. Feel free to read ahead.

For the record I will not apologize. I am not sorry for my feelings, nor am I sorry for the manner in which I express them. I am not sorry for the intermittent dropping of F-Bombs or for my unfiltered and sometimes explosive rage. I am not sorry for speaking candidly about my experiences with a certain person and a particular disease. I am not sorry for not being sorry. I accept and welcome with open arms the possibility that I may present as a bitter, hateful bitch. Whatever.

"Alcoholism is a disease! Would you be so cold if it were cancer?" Here's the deal. If someone has cancer, and a doctor informs them that, with treatment, they could make a full recovery, then the assumption would be that they would likely accept that treatment. If they don't get the help, that is entirely their own choice, but it is equally a loved one's choice to be angry. Especially when another human being's decision to essential kill themselves, kills other family members in many ways, as well. It's not the disease that pisses me off, it's the denial. Last I checked, substance abuse and selfishness, though often comorbid, are not a singular syndrome. Being sick and being a dick are two very separate issues.

Frankly, nobody gave a shit about whether I was upset or offended when my ex-husband was dismantling my life, piece by drunken piece so I'm just leveling the playing field for all of us happy hour housewives.

In an effort to organize my thoughts and effectively express my experience, I have asked myself scores of questions. Why did this happen? Am I right? Wrong? Weak? Strong? Stupid? Did I deserve this? Am I a good mom? A good woman? Am I even a decent human being? What could I have done differently? Where do I go from here? Can I keep going at all? Will I ever understand his pain? Will he ever understand mine? Will he ever show remorse? Does it even matter? What the fuck?!

All of these are excellent questions, but ones with insufficient answers. The answer is, and will always be, that there is no answer. What to do, how to survive, when to leave, who to trust, where to go are all cars in an interstate pileup with no exit in sight.

Upon visiting a local Alanon meeting in late 2005, I was finally given an answer to one of these essential questions. I listened patiently to three women discuss their bouts with the alcoholism of their husbands, children and parents. With increasing anxiety and diminishing tolerance, I eventually had the floor. I told my story, short and sweet, sprinkled with fucks and chuckles because that's my way. Then, like Ralphie blurting out his desperate desire for a BB gun, I unrepentantly asked, "What do I do now?" I asked this question seriously wanting an answer and foolishly believing there was one. I asked it bluntly and it was answered in the same fashion, with two of my very favorite things: levity and brevity. The woman chose her words carefully and, with a subtle tone insinuating that someday I'd be in on the joke, she handed me this ugly little pearl of wisdom. "You'll stay as long as you can deal with it, and when you can't deal with it any longer, you'll leave."

I was stunned. And super pissed. I came here for this? I dumped my purse on their table, told a group of strangers in a church basement the most embarrassing, intimate details of my current situation, and THAT is what they tell me? I think what truly enraged me was that, on some primal, molecular level, I knew this was the truth. This meeting did not provide me with an answer, a direction, a moment of clarity or even a sigh of relief. Not then.

I vividly remember smoking a cigarette on my ride home and talking out loud to myself about what a bunch of idiots these women were.

If I only knew then what I know now....

Levity and brevity. I have grown to appreciate her response for those two reasons. Simplicity is a virtue in my book, and there was an underlying humor that is only visible when you are far enough removed from when the joke is on you, and capable of laughing at it. To be honest, I don't even think she meant it to be funny, rather that she was sincere and felt sorry for me and my naiveté. I feel bad for that shadow of myself as well. But the world turns and the hits keep coming, and sometimes the best and only appropriate response is to laugh, even when it's not funny.

Growing up in an Irish Catholic family, one learns quickly that a too soon joke is often the best kind of funny. It allows you to laugh at something when you really feel like crying. The always entertaining crack at a wake or when someone's in the ICU, lends desperately needed comic relief to a sad state of affairs.

In any event, the questions always linger and the answers always evade, but we do the best we can to appease our egos and clear our consciences. I learned a great deal from my dabbling in Alanon. I learned about the disease, its effects on families, children, finances, friendships, and most other of life's most precious gifts. I learned about my ex-husband and his insatiable need for a total disconnect from this world, its beauty and its pain. I learned how much I had lost of myself in the storm of his disease, and how much I had to rebuild in its aftermath. In all the insanity, I had lost the answer to one question that at some point, in a distant life, I'd had an answer to. Who am I?

This seems to be such a basic concept but, when coping with another individual's issues, it's so terrifyingly simple to forget. It's easy to believe that it doesn't even matter.

But it does.

And here is my answer.

I am a writer. Mostly I write a lot of lists, checks, and cutting emails that I never send; but they're decisively pointed and crushing, I assure you. Writing is cathartic and empowering, and sometimes the only decent therapy one can afford. I reflect on some of my favorite authors: Dickenson, Gilman, Hemingway and Twain, and think "what a bunch of fucking nuts," but we all are in one way or another. So, in grand old Mark Twain tradition, I will begin with a warning, a notice to the reader.

This is NOT a self-help book. It will not be filed between Tony Robbins and Deepak Chopra. This is not a professional manual pertaining to substance abuse and alcoholism. I will not presume to have the clinical knowledge to regale you with the facts and figures, symptoms and side effects of this disease. It is not a reference book for divorce or a workbook on becoming a better you. This book is, however, an account of an all too common experience in dealing with an alcoholic. It is sometimes harsh, often sad and always real. Every single word of it is as real as it is unbelievable. And as a smooth segue to the following point, it comes with delicious drink recipes. You're welcome.

I am a bartender. Irony is fun! I am one of those sarcastic, make fun of my customers in a way they find endearing, bartenders. You may think I'm a bitch after you pay your tab, but you're coming back tomorrow for round two, trust and believe. I make a slamming drink too, by the way, especially my signature Bloody Mary. Bartending has helped me get through some exceedingly difficult years both financially and emotionally.

Though slinging drinks for eight hours while breastfeeding and having a nervous breakdown may not seem like a stellar night out to some people, it does afford a lonely, miserable mother of a young child certain monetary and social gains. It's like your friends paying to hang out with you because you make a pitcher of sangria for them. That said, in order to help me help you, I have included a handy adult beverage recipe to kick off each story in style.

While mixing bevvies may seem a largely inappropriate counterpart to trudging through someone else's substance abuse, let's be honest with each other. Someone else's habitual drinking and driving, really drives a person to drink.

I am a teacher. I moved on up from serving the special needs of adults by expediting their social lubrication, to teaching middle school special education students. Upgrade? Jury is still out. They say that those who can't do, teach. Those people are obviously not teachers, they're assholes. Teaching is an art. I can teach children to read and write. I can teach them the importance of having the ability and capacity to communicate effectively and with purpose. I can teach them to listen when they don't want to and to cope with their disabilities in the real world. I can teach them respect and boundaries and trust. I can do all of these things with these children because they have the courage to change the things they can, and the willingness to gain the wisdom to do so. I can do none of these things with a grown man who is resistant to all things in the progress department. Maybe, what I can teach him is a lesson.

I am a woman and, much to every man's dismay, we remember everything. On the rare occasion that memory serves insufficiently, we write that shit down and save it for a rainy day. Thus this compilation of years and tears, notes scribbled on post-its and envelopes, text messages sent to myself as reminders of terrible things I don't wish to be reminded of, but need to. Innumerable journal entries, diaries, court papers, AA logs, DYFS reports, risk assessments, police files, stacks and stacks of bills, more bills, emails from my son's school, and family photos with a certain someone crossed out in crayon. The list is boundlessly depressing and a driving force at once.

The beauty of being a woman is that despite all of this, we persevere. The strength within a woman provides us with the ability to overcome adversity, problem solve, multi-task, and keep it moving in general. Women not only possess an intrinsic master set of coping skills, we also take the opportunity to share our knowledge and pass it along. This exceptionally powerful, singularly female asset also comes in handy when life sends a big, steaming pile of bullshit our way with little to no regard for the lukewarm pile we are still cleaning up.

Such is why women bear children, and will eventually rule the Earth. One thing that the male readers, assuming there are any, will gain from this storytelling experience is the insight to understand what women have to deal with, and to know when they have had enough. A series of disgustingly unfortunate events has enabled me to perfect a certain "don't fuck with me" look. Please be advised, it's not just a look. It's a learned behavior and a lifestyle. Do not fuck with me.

I am a mother and I would do absolutely anything for my son. My sweet, innocent son, so undeserving of the deuce seven off suit hand his father has dealt him. He is an angel. Smart as a whip and funny as hell. He has the creative spark of a miniature artistic genius and signature dance moves that are unrivaled in entertainment value. He is my greatest source of joy and the reason I endure when I have lost all faith and desire to do so. I want him to have all the happiness that life can give. I want him to believe in himself and his dreams. I want to give him the best of everything as much and as often as I can.

My hope for him is that he learns each and every day, appreciates the importance of kindness and love, and helps and respects those who are different from him. I would like to believe that I am passing on some of these qualities down to him and that one day, he will know that I did the very best I could with what I had, and always placed his needs before my own. I want him to have a dad, and he doesn't. And no matter how much I want that for him, I can't make his dad want it too. I want to fix things for my son and, while I have fantasized about various ways to make that happen including the mafia and vehicular manslaughter, at the end of the day, there is nothing more I can do. The ball is in dad's court.

I am an alcoholic's anonymous ex. I am the nameless, faceless collateral damage of this disease. I am a million different people and nobody at once.

I must have been raking straw near the manger and dropped the baby Jesus on his head in a previous life to deserve this fun-filled experience. Anyone who has been there, and if you're reading this there is a piping hot chance you have, knows what I'm talking about. I know in my heart that there are far too many people that will relate to this story because it's all too common and it isn't funny.

My hope for my maniacal muse is that he reads this. Albeit in a likely alcohol induced, near blackout state, my hope is that he reads it and is mad as hell. I hope that he mother fucks me up and down and tears the book to shreds, indignantly asserting what a bitch liar I am. I hope then, that when he views his bloated, shadow of his former self, reflection in the mirror, that he startles into reality and hits bottom. I hope he finds sobriety, happiness and, above all else, a way to rebuild his relationship with his son. I hope that he finds the courage to fight his disease head on and defeat it, because the rest of us soldiers are either unwilling to fight for him, or have become casualties in his war.

Though I remain unapologetic for writing this memoir of a broken life, I am certain days will come when I question doing so. There will be guilt and all of the feelings associated with the grieving process as I reflect upon my own contributions to this substance tsunami that has all but destroyed our family. There will be moments when I will beat myself up for what I have done, what I didn't do, and what I could have done better. I will surely cry, for him, for me, and for our son as I have done so many times before. But I will not apologize. At the very least, I will reflect, one skill he has yet to master, or even attempt. Throughout all, of the varied stages of denial, acceptance and recovery related to dealing with an alcoholic, I have battled these emotional demons and I am convinced that I will continue to do so. I feel sorry for him but I will not be sorry. The situation is sorry. The behavior is sorry. He is sorry. I am not.

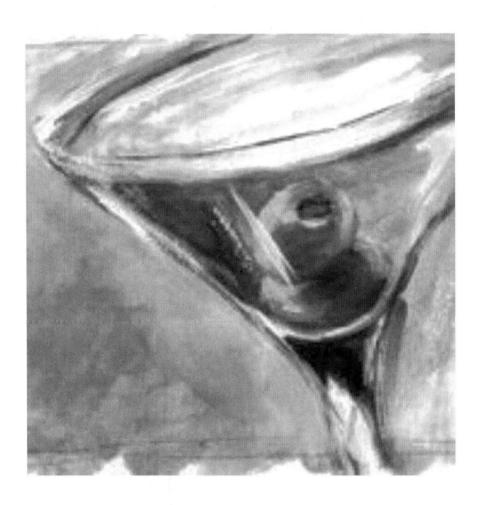

1: Straight Up

Classic Martini

The drink that never goes out of style, and can be tailored to your own taste as well as your budget.

2 ounces of your preferred vodka

A splash of dry vermouth

Your choice of garnish (olives, onions, twist of lemon, tears)

Pour vodka over ice and add dry vermouth sparingly. Cover and swirl glass to mix and cool. Strain into chilled martini glass. Add garnish.

Cheers.

To quote the ever-classy Coco Chanel, "I don't care what you think about me, I don't think about you at all." This fairly astutely sums up my outlook on people and the world at large. On some glorious day in my late twenties, when the clouds parted and the angels sang, I stopped giving a shit what other people thought. If you don't like me that's ok, I probably don't like you either.

Now, don't mistake my straightforward approach with rudeness or arrogance. I know that there are many people smarter, funnier, and richer, better looking and better at life than my little old self. Some people have a tendency to think they're better than others or to regularly point out when someone is worse off than they are. That's not how I roll. I do my thing, you do yours, and so long as my thing and your thing don't adversely affect each other, it's all good in the hood.

On another note, ever watch one of those commercials for injury lawyers that will win you a settlement if you have experienced any symptoms between breathing and death? There's no pot of gold at the end of this shit brown rainbow, but maybe some much needed comradery. In order to gain a comprehensive concept of what life is like with an alcoholic, I have graciously put together a little fact sheet for your enjoyment. If you have already had the distinct pleasure of intimately relating to an alcoholic, feel free to make check marks and make yourself another drink. If it wasn't straight up before, it probably will be now.

Have you ever:
-had to pick someone up at a police station?
-or at an out of state hospital?
-picked a car up from impound?

-wondered where all of the money has gone?

-wondered where your sanity has gone?

-found bottles hidden in the attic?

-the crawl space?

-the garage?

-the dresser?

-the backyard?

-been humiliated in front of your friends?

-your family?

-cleaned up after someone, that isn't your child, wet the bed?

-met with a divorce attorney?

-met with another divorce attorney?

-held on to divorce papers just hoping?

-filed for divorce?

-filed for bankruptcy?

-filed a DYFS report?

-filed for a temporary restraining order?

-hoped this was rock bottom?

-told yourself this was the last time?

If you've answered yes to any one or all of these questions, you may be suffering from alcoholism by-proxy. Side effects may include sadness, fatigue, weight gain or loss, headaches, nausea, trouble sleeping, rage and increased thoughts of suicide. If you are experiencing any one or more of these symptoms, please seek help. Remember the Alanon lady and her advice?

2: Open Bar

Suggested pairing: Sage Advice

My advice to you is to make a pitcher of this from the get-go because, chances are, you're going to need it.

Fresh blackberries

½ ounce lemon juice

1 teaspoon of sugar

2 ounces Jameson

Club Soda

Sage leaves and blackberries for garnish

Muddle berries, lemon juice and sugar in a rocks glass. Add ice and Jameson. Top off with club soda. Garnish with blackberries and sage leaves.

Cheers.

To My Son's Father,

While you truly do not deserve an ounce of my energy or a moment of my time, I am writing to you on behalf of our son and his unfulfilled desire to experience some glimmer of a healthy and functional relationship with his father. I use the term "our son" extremely loosely as your contribution to his existence extends nominally beyond nature into nurture, and yet this beautiful little boy still longs for your love.

Let me begin by introducing you to your child, seeing as you know nearly nothing about him and have had the privilege of spending what equates to less than a calendar day with him within the past year. Our son is divine perfection. He possesses a triumphant trifecta of courage, charisma and cuteness. His blue-green eyes are sparkling, and full of wonder and wit. It's astounding that so much personality can exist in a small body, and that a creature that still, on occasion, throws a wicked tantrum can also possess such an old soul.

This boy is a verbal marathoner, speaking, singing, laughing, questioning, and joking from the second his eyes open until his mind finally allows him, and me, to rest. His tendency toward the inquisitive is exhausting and awe inspiring. He marvels at the intricacies of the articulation of action figures and aspires to reach the various advanced skill levels of all things Lego. He is an avid action movie fan and video game aficionado, expressing a multi-faceted knowledge base including, but not limited to, story lines, character development and special effects. He, much like his uncles and much to my dismay, is a hard core electronic dance music enthusiast who will undoubtedly be in attendance at the 2023

Burning Man Festival in Black Rock City. Oh dear God, what am I in for….

This boy can dance. He has rhythm, which he most certainly did not inherit from his maternal genetic contribution. He feels the beat, even if it is an echo from his own drum, and dances like no one is watching. I revel in his individual expression and envy his utter disregard of others' judgements. He is light-years ahead of his third grade peers with regard to maturity and self-awareness. He. Is. Funny. How such a young individual can possess such a sharp tongue and affinity for sarcasm is beyond me and beyond entertaining. His comedy repertoire extends from potty humor to intricately layered plays on words. Compassion is a strong-suit as well. He empathizes with the plights of others and cares deeply for his family and furry friends. His hugs are many, cuddles generous and "I love you's" plentiful.

This earthly angel and ethereal spirit can sometimes fall from grace. He can be difficult and sometimes disrespectful. He has come a long, long way down a rough and winding road, but is still a majestic work in progress. Simple tasks like homework and showers can send him spiraling into rage. Often his predisposition towards being emphatic is to his detriment and my disappointment. Defiance is a word that seems suitable when discussing his willingness to cope with an unwanted outcome or complete an undesirable task. On evenings when I have regrettably extended his day ever slightly past bedtime, the overtired monster rears its ugly head and a battle of wills ensues. In the end, nobody wins.

This boy can be a master manipulator. He knows how to turn a situation upside down and make me feel like the bad guy. My buttons are frequently and accurately pushed, my nerves are shot and my conscience is commonly racked with guilt. He has learned that I have a penchant for overcompensation and he has developed a reciprocal propensity toward exploitation. He has an innate ability to make me question the fundamental difference between want and need, which inevitably leads me down a path of regret and an aisle in Toys R Us. It comes as no surprise that there exist varied negative behaviors as this beautifully clean slate has been written on by you, resulting in a diagnosis of clinical childhood depression and generalized anxiety. These character attributes in need of improvement are easily attributed to an external, paternal force.

I am well aware of your delusional misconception that the world revolves around you, so allow me to take a moment to address your favorite topic. You are an asshole. You deserve the title for the World's Greatest Asshole, in fact. In a world driven by selfishness and greed, you somehow manage to out-asshole everybody else. In the eight and a half glorious years that our child has graced this planet, you have managed to not only miss out on countless memories and milestones, but also to contribute a surplus of disappointment and daddy issues to his life.

Time and time again you have failed to show up, forgotten to call, and fucked with your son's emotions and sense of security. You have become famous for incoherent phone conversations and infamous for failing sobriety tests. You make zero attempt to support your child in any manner whatsoever. You take no initiative to be involved in his schooling. You take no steps to take part in his healing. You ignore all monetary obligation to assist in his surviving. You are an asshole.

I can't even fathom how you spend your time. Simple math tells me that in any given week there are 168 hours. I spend them all with our child. What on God's green Earth do you do? I know what you don't do. You don't put him on or take him off the bus. You don't feed him or clothe him or cuddle with him. You do not help him with his homework. You don't teach him to tie his shoes, or swim or ride a bike. You don't read to him. You don't comfort him. You don't care for him. There are moments that I question if you even love him. If you do, I am quite certain you do significantly less than you love yourself.

Despite you landing a walk-on role as an extra, and simultaneously winning the Academy Award for playing the irreverent douchebag dad, I must confess, I am thankful to you for many things. The first, and most obvious, is for contributing your genetic material to create him, albeit the solitary shining achievement of your legacy in fatherhood. Secondly, I would like to extend my sincerest gratitude for the many lessons you have taught our boy.

Thank you for teaching him to be strong. Without your constant onslaught of spectacular fuck ups, he might not be as fiercely resilient as he is today. Had you not failed him in every way imaginable, he might have only had the opportunity to be a typical little boy.

Thank you for teaching him to be independent. He doesn't need you. Not for anything anymore. He explores on his own and learns on his own every single day. He has become such a phenomenally independent learner, in fact, when he thought your voice sounded "droopy" (as he called it) on the phone, he googled "side effects of being drunk," all by himself. Aren't you proud?

Thank you for teaching him one of life's most valuable lessons: expect nothing and you'll never be disappointed. I'll be damned if he doesn't know that for sure. Thank you for teaching him how to cope with grief, and anxiety, and depression at such an early age. You've certainly reared a child ahead of his time. Thank you also for all of the unsolicited advice you continue to dole out to your son: he should play a sport, he should eat more vegetables, he should be thinner, faster, smarter, better.

Since you seem so interested in working in the advice department, allow me to return the favor.
Get a job.
Get a life.
Get a grip on your selfish, self-serving and petulant behavior.
Get it together for your son.

There is an old adage that states "anyone can be a father, but it takes someone special to be a daddy." My dad has a framed print with that saying on it; a gift he received from his children. You don't, and you never will. See, you're not special because there are thousands of deadbeat dads just like you, and you all blow.

Our son is special. He is smart and funny and all-around awesome, and when he grows up, he'll be like me — tough, independent and successful. He'll have a spectacular sense of humor and well-rounded sense of self. He'll have a college degree, a career and a family. He'll have the world at his fingertips and he'll have you to thank for none of it.

So Sincerely,
Your Son's Mother

3: Old Fashioned

Suggested pairing: Bourbon Old Fashioned

You know, because I'm an old fashioned bitch.

2 ounces Bourbon Whiskey

Dash of Bitters

Dash of water

1 teaspoon sugar

1 Maraschino cherry

1 orange wedge

Combine sugar, bitters and water in a glass. Add fruit and muddle into a thick paste. Fill with ice and add bourbon.

Cheers.

I resent being referred to as a single parent. I view it as a dated, insufficient, and inappropriate term for the majority of people it is used to describe. The expression, "single parent" does not in any manner reflect the description of the responsibilities and hardships many people stereotyped as such endure. The title of single parent is old fashioned and, much like its liquor counterpart of the same name, may be sweet, but it is inevitably hard to swallow.

"Oh, she's such a hard worker being a single parent, and all," they say. "It must be so difficult supporting her son without any help." Yeah, no shit. It is hard, and as passively condescending as people may intend to be in typecasting you as a single parent, let me be very clear. The title is one that is inherently muddled by all of the gray area and bullshit that accompany it, and over time it becomes rather offensive.

When the counterpart to your parenting responsibilities is a self-centered, near-sighted jackass of a human being, who is solely focused on satiating the addict within him, you become solely focused upon survival-yours and your child's. To add insult to injury, you are not only required to pick up the pieces of your own existence and keep it moving, you have to do so double time for your kids. There is no break, no vacation, not even a time out. You barely get a chance to rage and grieve one insanity inducing event before, toot toot, the crazy train pulls into the station with a new one. It is a lifestyle that is equal parts struggle and strength. Since the job description is vague and all encompassing, I have provided a handy definition for you to refer to. It seems only fitting that since the parent is double, the definition is as well.

Double Parent (n)

1. An individual who is responsible for the physical, emotional and financial well-being of their offspring without the assistance of the respective co-parent, due to that person's self-centered, narcissistic, substance abusing bullshit behavior

2. An individual who inadvertently acquires an additional child, one who used to be an adult, but refuses to act like one (see also: dickhead, man-child)

By definition, you are alone with only your wits and determination to keep you going. Your partner in parenting has regressed to childhood and you are expected to gracefully move forward as they pathetically stumble back without remorse. It is a bizarre linear equation wherein, as positive as you become as a role model, they become equally negative. You are left to manage every potentially disastrous circumstance, finance each monetary obligation and field all questions, comments, complaints and statements including, but not limited to:

"Can I have this?"

"What does this mean?"

"Am I allowed to?"

"Can I go to (fill in the blank)?"

"You're the worst."

"Why can't I?'

"I hate you."

"I like my dad better than you."

"My dad is the best."

"Why won't YOU let me see him?"

"I wish I lived with my dad and not you."

"Mom, why?"

"Mom, help."

"Mom, wait."

"Mom, please?"

"Mom?"

"Mom!"

"MOM!!!!!! Are you listening?"

Are YOU listening? You are not a single parent, not when you are required to respond to all of these questions without a second set of ears, and react to them without a second set of hands. YOU are a double parent.

We do both jobs. Mom and Dad. Good cop, bad cop. Family, friend. It is as exhausting as it is unrelenting. This job does not give a shit if you are tired, broke, cranky, sad, scared or fed up. It is the life sentence of parenting, without the possibility of parole. There is no resignation, no quitting, because if we can take anything at all positive from our addict it is not to be a quitter. Seems like a double-edged mantra, now that I think about it. It is an offense to impose onto someone this lifelong position and it is offensive to refer to them in a manner that demeans them by slicing their contribution in half, in just the label alone.

In the world of addiction, a single parent is a unicorn. It is a beautiful, mythical creature that eats candy and shits rainbows. It is kind and forgiving, and knows no negativity. It doesn't exist. Co-parenting with an addict is no singular feat. There is nothing single about this occupation, save for the fact that you most likely are, at least in the relationship department. You may have been the elusive single parent for a shining, naive moment at the start, but eventually the stress, workload, and resentment compounds thus morphing the single parent unicorn into a dark, double parent demon. While the unicorn flits from cloud to cloud, embracing the glitter and giggles life has to offer, the demon spits fire and spews venom at the universe that twisted its fate into the ugliness it has become.

The single to double evolution occurs when the reality slowly seeps in and you awaken to the truth that every aspect of life that was supposed to be joint, shared, split down the middle, has been dumped in your lap like a child with a dirty diaper. The single parent explodes and grows stronger, faster, smarter and better while its adversary cowers in fear and shame. Their only weapons are deflection and manipulation, and while they are masters in the sport, they prove no match for the demon's determination.

Now, the double parent is not evil as demons often present. They are merely angels that have fallen into a hell of someone else's design. They were once happy, optimistic creatures that existed in a world of beauty and possibility. Sadly and unpredictably, they are exiled into a darkness, a bottomless pit that has no end, no light, and seemingly no cohabitants. There is vast, undeniable loneliness, for who would choose to exist in this blackness and obscurity? How could anyone possibly fathom a life so disconnected from the world that once was?

You fade into the night, succumb to the insanity, and accept the unacceptable. It is a deep, dark abyss but, unlike the hole the addict resides in, there is a bottom, and there is a top. The most important of the countless duties of a double parent is to find it. There may exist a labyrinth of dead ends, dark paths and doors to nowhere, but there is an exit. You owe yourself, and your children that journey back out.

As long as there is an active substance abuser, there will be a double parent. We will provide everything to ensure our children's survival and success. Food. Clothing. Hugs. Kisses. Shoulders. Shelter. Haircuts. School supplies. Movie nights. Cuddles. Laughs. Structure. Support. Homework help. Playdates. Toys. Sneakers. Sports. Discipline. Boundaries. Day care. Doctors. Understanding. Sympathy. Empathy. Acceptance. Tolerance. Love. Love. Love. Not to be outdone, the addict will provide for our children as well. Disappointment. Tears. Fear. Resentment. Sadness. Inconsistency. Anger. Rage. Confusion. Anxiety. Depression.

Weighing the contributions by both parties is like drawing a really fucked up Venn diagram. It's excessively uneven and offensive to the senses. It's a mathematical equation with so much carrying, too many unknowns, and innumerable variables, making it impossible to solve. You would require the "Beautiful Mind" of ugly situations to crack this bitch. The answer to double parenting, similar to the answer to dealing with an addict, is that there really is no answer.

You are the only answer. I was the answer, it just took me many years and too many tears to figure that out. Someone incredibly insightful once told me that when I'm doing better, my son is doing better. They were unquestionably right. There is absolutely nothing we can do to fix another person if they lack the desire and the drive to do it for themselves, for their children. What we can control is how we choose to cope with their behavior, how to react and respond to it. I can spend my days bitter and angry, brooding about what could have been and what is, but the only destination lying at the end of that path is a dead end, and he would be there waiting, because that is where he chooses to exist. I refuse to be like him. I resolve to be better than that, for me and for my son. So in a world overflowing with demons, unicorns, substance abusers and double parents, make me a double. The hangover may be rough but the pleasure is worth the pain. I would choose doing twice as much to be a parent than to not be one at all. I may be old fashioned, but if you have a child you can't be a child. Shut up, grow up, suck it up and keep it moving.

4: Tom Collins

Suggested pairing: Vodka Collins

Please chug all beverages and secure tray tables prior to takeoff.

It's going to be a bumpy ride. Godspeed.

2 ounces vodka

2 ounces lemon juice

1 ounce simple syrup

1 dash bitters

Club soda

Lemon wedge

Fill cocktail shaker with ice. Add vodka, lemon juice, simple syrup and bitters. Shake until thoroughly combined and chilled. Pour contents into highball glass and top with club soda. Garnish with lemon wedge.

Cheers.

In the spirit of all things "Throwback Thursday" and "Flashback Friday," allow me to introduce you to something I like to call "Shitfaced Saturday." Sit back and relax with a fanciful concoction, and join me on my journey back through space and time.

Every experience with an alcoholic or an addict is insanity inducing in its own way. While each circumstance maintains its own flair for fucked up and knack for knocking you over, most come down to one basic, fundamental truth. The truth of the matter is that there is no truth in the matter. Like a hound dog sniffing out a scent, a seasoned partner has a hypersensitivity to sensing bullshit.

The inherent problem with this is that, once hot on the trail of a big, fat lie, the path veers off in many directions, all of which chase down another deception. With each layer of bullshit uncovered, a new, even more disturbing layer is revealed. Questions produce questions and typically provide us with little more than aggravation and exhaustion.

Sometimes we ignore the lie. Sometimes we pursue the truth. And sometimes, we ante up to the irrationality and go big or go home. Winter 2007. Baby's first Christmas. One full year into his relapse. A chill was in the air, and a deep freeze in our marriage. Great time to plan a party. Shortly before the scheduled holiday extravaganza, my ex left on an ill-timed business trip to Virginia, and I was left with a bag of burning shit. A house to clean. Food to prepare. Decorations to display. A Christmas tree to purchase, put up, and decorate. Two dogs. A baby. And a partridge in a pear tree.

To an extent, I begrudged the constant travel and incessant golf outings, but I mostly sucked it up because it was his employment that paid our bills. This particular pill was a harder one to swallow because of the burden of preparing to host upwards of forty people in our home, while simultaneously carrying a crying baby on my hip. Do you know how difficult it is to sweep floors one-handed? Not to mention how ridiculous it must've looked.

The excursion lasted roughly four or five days, my memory fails me as to the precise number – but it was a long, arduous week for me, nonetheless. The icing on the fruitcake of this trip was that his return flight had been delayed, and my long awaited relief had been as well. Beyond frustrated, I logged into the Continental Airlines website and clicked on the "check flight status" icon so that I could determine the exact moment in time I could anticipate his arrival. I'd had it. I needed a break. Five fucking minutes of quiet to down a glass of wine and decompress. Five minutes not holding, feeding, burping, rocking, swaddling, bathing, soothing, and mothering a child. A few, glorious, God forsaken moments without sweeping, scrubbing, cooking, wrapping, decorating, planning, organizing, or worrying.

"Flight arrived early."

Estimated time listed.

Actual time listed.

Gate number listed.

You have got to be fucking kidding me. I sat and pondered exactly what this could mean. I reviewed the itinerary and attempted to determine what was going on and how to proceed. I remained silent. Until he got home. Drunk. It was high time to heed Bowie's advice to "take your protein pills, and put your helmet on."

"Where were you?" I asked calmly.

"What do you mean, where was I?" he responded in the same fashion. "My flight got delayed and I had to wait for a cab to get home."

What really pisses me off in a conversation such as this is the outright indignant way in which he belittles my question, and insinuates that I am, in fact, the crazy one. A tidal wave of rage surged within me, and I began firing off pointed questions as to his whereabouts. I erupted and he shrugged me off, staggering into another room in an attempt to evade my interrogation. I persisted. I engaged in a real-life game of Beer Pong wherein the drunker you are, the more cups you sink. The anxiety and rage had knocked me off my game. I was missing all of my shots while he sank cup after cup, re-racking into diamond formation as my game grew erratic and haphazard.

I couldn't think straight so I retreated. I had a drink. I smoked a cigarette. I phoned a friend. I regrouped and reminded myself that I am the rational one here. I am right. I am determined. And so I persevered.

When confronting an alcoholic's dishonesty head on, one eventually finds themselves at an intersection of two avenues of insanity. There is the addict's path, twisted and endless, littered with defiance and denial. Then, at a crossroads of catharsis, there lies ours. It is a bumpy road, riddled with detours and bad neighborhoods, but it is the road to righteousness. We must follow this path to its end and seek the truth, whatever that may be.

The path that evening was extensive and exasperating. I took turns at phone calls and websites and family, and each and every detour led me back to the same place – Bullshit Boulevard. I acknowledge that at a certain point, my crazy, while sober and justified, eventually rivaled his intoxicated insanity. I knew he was lying but some sick, self-indulgent need existed within me to uncover the truth about this trip.

I paced the house. I checked the website again. I confronted him with the flight status information. "It's wrong," he said. "They made a mistake," he insisted. Of course they're wrong. I'm wrong. Continental Airlines is wrong. Everyone is wrong and he is right. I should have anticipated this response.

I called Newark Airport. I spoke with customer service representatives and supervisors and everyone in between. After hours, yes hours, on the phone with various innocent bystanders left to field my frustration, I spoke with an Air Traffic Control officer. Air. Traffic. Control. My convolution required this level of expertise to confirm something I already knew undeniably to be true. They kindly, albeit somewhat condescendingly, explained to me the liability and legality behind providing accurate flight information to the public. They regaled me on FAA regulations and flight status protocols. They told me that it would be irresponsible and ILLEGAL to post inaccurate flight data. Illegal. I had my smoking gun.

"I just spent two hours on the phone with the airport and the airline and they told me that there is NO POSSIBLE WAY your flight was in the air when you said it was! So, where were you?!!" I shot at him with anger and rage, disgust and disbelief. Bang, bang motherfucker!

"I don't know what you want from me," he said.

"I want the fucking truth!"

"I wasn't in Virginia, I was in New York City. I needed to go out and have fun for a few days."

And just like that, he shot me back.

Whether it is woman's intuition, or a gut instinct, or a sixth sense, when it comes to an alcoholic, where there's smoke, there's always fire. Beneath each truth is something false. There are often layers upon layers of lies and denial, so many, we may never uncover them all. But do we really want to?

My mother, in all of her infinite wisdom, reminds me not to ask a question if I don't really want the answer. Did I want to know? What did I gain from this? I told you so? I was right and you were wrong? I'm smarter than you think? The truth hurt as much as the lie, to be completely honest.

It is painful and thankless to play drinking games with drinkers. They always win, even when they lose. This felt like a game of Asshole, and I inevitably was the asshole. Truth or lie, it is a lose-lose situation when you are playing against someone who doesn't know when to quit.

He engaged me in his crazy game for hours that night. He belittled my feelings, denied my accusations and sidestepped my questions. It hurts deeply when someone holds you in such a low regard that they will lie to your face without hesitation. Your pain means nothing. Your concerns are irrelevant. Your trust is broken.

Despite feeling like the "crazy one," I am confident I am not. I refuse to play Asshole, and I rarely lose at Beer Pong. True story. I may have traveled dark paths of weakness and indecision, but I tour those roads no more. It is his dysfunction, not mine.

YOUR circuit's dead, there's something wrong

Can you hear me, Major Tom?

Can you hear me, Major Tom?

Can you hear me, Major Tom?

5: Happy Hour

Suggested pairing: Pitcher of Pink Sangria

Why have a pint when you can have a whole pitcher?

1 bottle Rose Wine

¼ cup Brandy

¼ cup Peach Schnapps

½ cup Triple Sec

2 cups cranberry juice

2 cups ginger ale

Raspberries, strawberries and red grapes

Procure large beverage vessel and combine all ingredients, except ginger ale. Add fresh fruit and chill overnight. Once chilled, add ginger ale and serve in stemless wine glasses.

Cheers.

Happy Hour, as I have come to understand it, is a short, splendid respite from the stress of everyday life. A beautifully brief period meant to cohort with colleagues and play with peers. Essentially, it is a play date for grown-ups. Adult amusement. A big deal for big people. But, let us not forget the small people we sometimes seek solace from. The miniature maniacs, and the "minor" aggravations. These young people yearn for a happy hour of their own. They long for interaction, imagination and instant gratification.

Children, as deeply as they love their parental counterparts, crave interactive experiences that are exclusive to their elementary community. Social interaction at an early age is essential in building the foundation of a healthy, well-rounded adult. Our ability to function within a society by sympathizing, empathizing and nurturing the needs of those beyond ourselves is a skill that is established by the ways in which we relate to our childhood friends. So what if our children don't know how to do this?

My child does not play like other children. He employs intellect over athletics, sarcasm over sleepovers, and independence over interaction. He is not an athlete, refuses to ride a bike, and despises summer camp. My son is easily frustrated and exhibits a noticeable degree of social anxiety. There is an overtone of negativity, underscored by a persistent defeatist attitude. His immediate response to a situation is often to lash out or to presume the worst possible outcome. He cycles through various nervous tics and perseverates on collecting: Pokémon cards, action figures, Legos. Past meltdowns have persisted for the better part of an evening, involved destruction of possessions and self-injury, and have required physical intervention, psychiatric evaluation and mobile response assistance. At the height of his diagnosed clinical depression, comorbid with anxiety and rage, he has threatened to jump from a moving vehicle, pulled out his hair and even alluded to suicide. He was five at the time. Five. Five. Years. Old. He is the product of an exceptionally poor roll of the dice of parental circumstance, one who has to bluff a shitty hand, hoping the other players don't discover his poker face.

Can you blame him?

Until recently, I awoke each morning with the same thought, the same hope, and the same wish. Please let today be better than yesterday. Please let him wake up in a decent mood. Please let the breakdown be shorter and less violent. Please, please let him be happy.

From the ages of 4 and 7, the good days were few and far between. I cried happy tears when the clouds parted and my child saw sunshine. His sadness had become so severe, and his depression so deep, I wasn't sure he would ever find his way out. These years were filled with therapists, trips to the principal's office, and Child Study Team meetings. They were filled with rage and disappointment. They were so full because they were so empty.

I write about my own pain regarding his father's alcoholism but my hurt is the far lesser of the two evils. A child's suffering is the single most heart-wrenching experience a parent can endure. Witnessing a child aching for the unattainable and wanting for the one thing they can't have, the one thing they deserve most, is enough to shatter you into a million pieces.

But it cannot. We must keep going – especially for them. I must set the example. I will be strong and confident, so that he may learn to do the same. Despite the fact that he has the devastating pairing of only child and no-dad syndromes, he will always have a mother who loves him and never gives up.

None of us have perfect children. Some people pretend to but they are full of shit and we all know it. We have children with Autism, trauma, physical disabilities and communication impairments. We have babies who have behavioral and emotional issues, social deficits and learning disabilities. But we have children, and we are all so fortunate. And they are all perfect in their own way.

I qualified these struggles with the preface of "until recently" because there is an ever-present light at the end of the tunnel. It may be dim at times but it exists.

My son learned to swim. He has made neighborhood friends and plays with them functionally and frequently. He has established coping skills. He hasn't been to the principal's office since September. He does chores and homework. He sleeps in his room, goes to bed without incident and rarely has nightmares. He builds, he draws, he creates and he imagines. He discusses the spectrum of articulation pertaining to action figures, and researches the biographical information about his favorite actors. He thinks philosophically, jokes sarcastically and dances ridiculously.

His comebacks are quick and witty and his robot dance is kick-ass. He accepts the circumstances surrounding his father and expects little. He calls him, even when it consistently goes unanswered. He talks about his feelings. He laughs and smiles. He cozies with me on the couch. He tells me he loves me. He is perfectly beautiful.

Every hour will not be happy hour when it comes to parenting – for the parents or for the children, but every hour will be worthwhile. There is no last call when it comes to being a mommy. It is our duty to teach and to nurture, to empathize and endure, to be strong and overcome. We cannot ever give up, because if we accept defeat, we accept it for our children as well – and that is unacceptable.

There will be long, exhausting, unforgiving and unbelievably shitty hours, but there will be happy hours too. I will never give up. My son already has one parent that will teach him that. I will not succumb to the suffering, I will not submit to the stress. There will come days when it all seems too much, and the ability to continue comes into question, but I will not surrender.

We must all stand strong and look adversity in the eyes. We must laugh at it and say, "You fucked with the wrong person." We must never forget how strong we are, how far we've come, and the beautiful journey that lies ahead. So, when you stop and think you can do it no more, stop and think of the ones you are doing it for. And have a fucking glass of Sangria.

6: Overserved

Suggested pairing: Stella Artois

A beer as old as alcoholism, I'd imagine, dating back to 1366 in Belgium. Stella, meaning star in Latin, will make you feel like just that after consuming a few too many.

Cheers.

"A man can fail many times, but he isn't a failure until he begins to blame somebody else," says American naturalist, John Burroughs. It's tough to argue with that kind of basic, idiot-proof logic, in my opinion.

We all fail at one time or another, and in one way or another, but the vast majority of us are not failures. I think it takes a pretty substantial history of fuck ups to deem an individual a total disaster, but one could certainly merge into the EZ pass lane to failure once they begin projecting blame onto others.

Shortly after my son was born, I returned to the ever-fulfilling duty of tending bar, this time at a centuries-old stagecoach stop turned tap room, where the pours were substantial and so were the regulars. The bar was minimalist, seating at most 12 patrons in a quiet corner of the restaurant, but the selection of spirits was vast and awe-inspiring. There were always a half dozen delicious micro-brews on tap and a martini list that would make James Bond proud. For as many beverage choices as appeared on the menu, there was an equal or greater quantity of regular customers.

Over time, I got to know each by name and, more importantly, by drink. I also became all too familiar with each person's personality, drunk and sober, as well as their tip regiment. Eventually, the excitement wore off, the conversation became stale and the income stagnant. Occasionally, however, the cloud of consistency would part, and a newbie would roll in.

A handful of weeks into my new gig, I had the pleasure of serving a couple whom I had not yet met. They were local by residence, but stemmed respectively from differing east coast locales, she from Staten Island, he from Ohio or Pittsburgh (I always forget), though his accent indicated a more southern descent.

Upon initial introductions, they presented as friendly and outgoing but, more importantly, fluent in my dialect of sarcasm. So far, so good. I served up bottles of Stella and humor until we were all lit and laughing, and then we called it a night. They returned days later in good spirits, and seeking them. But not before having a few words for me.

I greeted them cheerfully, as cheerfully as I ever am, and presented them with menus, but there was an issue. "I was overserved the last time I was here, and I wanted to know what you were going to do about that," he said jokingly. I responded in kind, "I'm not going to serve you anymore," I told him, and I walked away.

"Well, that's not what I meant! I didn't mean I didn't want to be served!" He continued on as his wife and I relished in his own joke biting him in the ass, and I eventually came around and brought him an ice cold beer.

These particular regulars are wonderful people, two of the kindest most generous individuals I have had the pleasure of meeting, and we are great friends and still laugh about it today. A rare silver lining in the service industry.

In bartending, as well as many other occupations, there is a ridiculous amount of blame tossed about. "How could you run out of my favorite vodka?" people would ask, as though I had chugged the entire bottle intentionally, in a spiteful effort to ruin their evening. "But I was looking forward to the tuna special! Why didn't you tell me it might sell out?" as if my psychic abilities had failed me in the entrée department. "You should have cut me off." "You didn't tell me I had a tab before I walked out." "Why didn't you make me eat something?"

At least "I was overserved" was laced with humor and not deflection like all of the other absurd remarks.

Being a single mom, I get blamed for a lot of shit, but I can take it when it comes from an eight-year-old.

Monday morning and there's school. My fault.
Ran out of apple juice because he drank it all. My fault.
It's raining, can't go swimming. My fault.
McDonald's put a girl toy in the happy meal. My fault.
Dogs are barking. My fault.
Bloody nose. My fault.
Legos broke. My fault.
Lost "special coin" in the lawn. My fault.
Dad's an asshole. My fault.
Hot out. My fault.
Cold out. My fault.
It's a day that ends in y. My. Fucking. Fault.

I get it. Being a mom makes everything our fault by default because a negative consequence couldn't possibly be the result of negative behavior, and the remainder of the universe is somehow controlled by us, and we just fuck it up all the time on purpose to piss off our kids.

As the emotional equivalent to an eight-year-old, my ex has deflected an excessive and irrational volume of blame in my direction as well. No matter how royally he fucks up and how close he comes to having bought the farm, this scapegoat always gets kicked in the ass.

He has accused me of many bat-shit crazy things in the past. According to him, I married him and had his child in an elaborate scheme to acquire his money, or lack thereof. I have purposely and maliciously withheld our son in an effort to destroy their relationship for my own personal gain. I was accused of causing my ex's alcoholism, despite the fact that he'd been active in AA a decade before meeting me.

I have exaggerated the home and health effects of massive floods in our marital residence. I invented the black mold and inflated the asthma. I stole his dishes when I moved. (They were clean and dry in the dishwasher, by the way, but he wouldn't think to look there) I took the dogs from him, even though he repeatedly refused to care for them. I have caused his many ghosts-of-girlfriends-past to end relationships with him. I have tampered with alcohol swab tests in an effort to falsely implicate him. He assured my son's therapist that I am a drug addict, and "way worse than he's ever been." He even, on one occasion, accused me and my divorce attorney of breaking into his apartment and stealing important paperwork. Wow, really?

If these statements were even partially within the realm of reality, I would be an absolute failure of a human being. But remember what Burroughs says about failure...

I blame myself for plenty of things. I'm not always as good of a mom as I strive to be. I lose patience and get frustrated. I overcompensate for what my son's father does not do. Sometimes I miss out on time with my son because I'm tired and go to bed too early. Sometimes I miss out on time with my friends because I arrive late or leave early, mostly because I'm somewhat antisocial and didn't really want to go to begin with. I blame myself for enough of my own shortcomings, I don't need that supplemented with someone else's

So, the next time my ex, or anyone else for that matter, attempts to make me the scapegoat for their own bullshit, don't blame me when this scapegoat bites you in the ass. I did not overserve you, you drank too much. I did not withhold my son from you, you drank too much. I did not take from you or steal from you, you drank too much. I did not make your girlfriends break up with you or get you fired from your job, you drank too much.

I did not ruin your life. You. Drank. Too. Much.

7: Blackout Drunk

Suggested pairing: Mind Eraser

You'll be thankful you won't remember.

2 ounces Vodka

2 ounces Kahlua

2 ounces Tonic Water

Fill a rocks glass with ice. Layer ingredients beginning with the Kahlua, then vodka, and top with tonic water. Using a straw, drink entire shot starting from the bottom up.

Cheers.

Let's take a trip down memory lane, shall we? Thanks to Google Maps, and journals in this particular instance, we are equipped to make the journey, even if we do require a small amount of assistance. While the drive down this road becomes more difficult with age, the destination is ever-present. Even if we ignore the signs and pretend it isn't there.

In one of my ex's shining shitfaced moments, he managed to destroy our family car and my respect for him, all in one fell swoop. One evening, a weeknight might I add, about six years ago and a lifetime behind me, he was up to his regular nightly shenanigans, performing his destructive duties as a regular at a local bar. The bar was a subsequent stop after a full day of drinking on the golf course so, by then, the heat and the hedonism had surely gone to his head. Certainly, the multiple martini nightcaps only made matters worse. I was completely unaware that he had tipsily traipsed his way over to another establishment.

Like most occasions, he hadn't received any of my calls or text messages (so weird, right?), and I was left, like so many nights, just waiting. Waiting for a call. Waiting for THE call. Waiting for this to be over – in whatever manner that so happened. I got the call, from him, shortly after 11pm and it wasn't at all what I expected. It never was. Shame on me, I guess.

"I hit a telephone pole. A deer jumped out and I swerved to avoid it." Always the saint. What a guy, huh? Destroying his own vehicle to save some poor drunken doe that had been staggering across the street, on her way home from the Buck Bar. You must be fucking kidding me. I'm not sure what was more absurd; the fact that he was dumb enough to do this, or dumb enough to think I would believe it. He crashed the car. He lied about it. Not one to be outdone, the selfish and stupid did not stop there. He was going for a hammered hat trick.

I am an absolute fool. I'm just going to put that out there before I explain why.

Upon his wrecked request, I went and picked him up, with my then toddler in tow. As surely as he was heavily intoxicated, I was profoundly under the influence of him. So, off we went, and at the end of this specific memory lane, was a totaled car and an even more annihilated driver. So what did I do? I fucking panicked and drove him home. I was sober and probably more clouded in judgement than he was. His alcoholism had a way of doing that to me. Much like the car in the ditch, I almost couldn't discern which way was up anymore. God forgive me for letting my young child see something like this. Thank the Lord he doesn't have any memory of it. Sadly, he has too many other terrible memories of his dad to fill that space.

I mentioned this was a hat trick. Score! He smashed the car to pieces. Snuck another one past the goalie when he tried to blame it on Bambi. But here's the shot that hit home the hardest. When the police arrived, and they arrived in style — 4 State Trooper squad cars, lights and sirens to boot — his determination and delusion rose to a level of dick I was unaware even existed.

As he cowered in my son's nursery, wasted and worried, he asked me, in all seriousness, to tell the cops that I was the one driving the car. I shit you not. I may be a fool but I'm not an asshole. Even after I turned down this once in a lifetime offer, he proceeded to tell the officers himself, while handcuffed to a cute bistro chair on the front porch, that I was, in fact, driving the car, and he was home with our son. Oh. My. God. Long story short, he was arrested. Lost his license for a second time, and lost my respect forever.

Truth be told, I had forgotten about parts of this story until I began reading through old journals recently. I am certain he has managed to forget it too, whether by denial or deterioration. Maybe I chose to forget, maybe the corners of my mind were clouded with so much sadness that I closed them off and vowed to not revisit. Maybe both, but just because the memory isn't at the forefront of my mind, does not mean it never happened.

I am far from perfect. I get angry, I make mistakes and I curse like a truck driver, but that's me. I embrace those qualities, just as I embrace all of my missteps and misfortunes, because those are what pave the road from memory lane to me, today. I like who I am today because I choose to remember, even as he chooses to forget. He can have his spirits and his spite, because I have my spirit and my might, and that is what helps me to keep on truckin'. The path may be unclear, and I may sometimes walk it alone, but at least one of us is on the road to recovery.

8: Bottoms Up

Suggested pairing: Makers & Ginger with a Lime

My favorite person's favorite bevvie. Because even bullshit is better in good company.

2 ounces Makers Mark Bourbon

Ginger Ale

Wedge of Lime

Pour Makers over ice in pint glass or traveler, depending upon your destination. Fill with ginger ale and garnish with lime.

Cheers!

My little guy is the quintessential underdog in this game of life that his father has relentlessly and religiously been cheating at. My poor son is matched against an opponent who disobeys the rules, disrespects the players and disregards the object of the game. The odds are perilously stacked against my boy and, recently, he has become disinclined to play. I don't fucking blame him.

Occasionally, player number two reaches out and asks to speak with his son. Let's define occasionally, shall we?

I occasionally get to sleep past six in the morning. I occasionally eat Kentucky Fried Chicken. I occasionally see a movie that isn't a Disney Pixar film. Occasionally, as I see it, is reserved for shit that, although we would love to do more, just doesn't fit into our everyday schedules. I don't believe that parent/child interaction falls into this category. In any event, the sporadic incidences in which my ex reaches out are more and more frequently being met with the elementary school version of the middle finger.

"Your dad is home tonight and asked if you would give him a call."
"Never. He's the worst."
Amen to that.

Although I encourage him to remain in contact with his father, circumstances have evolved to the point where he has lost the desire to maintain a relationship with him, largely due to the fact that the relationship they have is total crap to begin with.
"Why don't you give your dad a call?"
"I don't want to."

"I don't want to" seems to be a fairly appropriate response to our current state of affairs. "I don't want to" seems to accurately reflect the status of my son's relationship with his father. "I don't want to" has a time and a place, and this is it.

Unfortunately, I've been inundated with what feels like a resounding, universal echo of "I don't want to" from all corners of my world and, for some irritating reason, this somewhat arbitrary and rather juvenile sense of reasoning is reserved for other people. Not me and, sorry to disappoint, but probably not you either.

When I'm not busy being a single mother I have the distinct honor and pleasure of spending my time with teenagers. There is no demographic that quite compares to adolescents. Many of us have one, we all were one and none of them, not even us, were fun. They are like miniature television commercial lawyers, making up for what they lack in expertise with a profound ability to argue anything at all, presenting a case devoid of any logic or reason. The teen trump card, like my son's anti-dad stance, is "I don't wanna" followed closely by "I can't" and, despite explaining the difference between can't and won't until I'm blue in the face, I'll be damned if those aren't their go-to forms of non-compliance.

Writing assignment? "I don't wanna."
Read a chapter in a book? "I can't."
Homework? "I can't, because I don't wanna."

While this line of reasoning can sometimes push me very near to the edge, it is a fairly typical teenaged mentality. I totally get that they don't want to but, eventually, they come around to the fact that they have to. So, I let it slide. For them. Adults, on the other hand, at least those who act like adults, do not have the option to not want to.

I don't know about you, but I think it's pretty safe to say that my electric company really doesn't give a shit if I don't want to pay my bill. When my son is hungry for dinner, it doesn't really matter if I don't want to cook anything. I don't want to do dishes or laundry or taxes for that matter, and I can say with absolute certainty that the IRS gives zero fucks about what I want, or don't want to do.

I read recently in the news that Kanye West is employing the "I can't" rationale to his fifty some-odd million-dollar debt. Evidently, he "can't" continue to grace us with his lyrical genius and fashion forward style without some assistance from the general public. In fact, there is a GoFundMe account in existence to help get poor Mr. West back on his feet and onto his high horse.

Now, I've been making a serious and concerted effort lately to keep my rage from boiling above a low simmer, but this is the kind of shit that incenses me. I sincerely doubt that the words can't or won't came rapping out of Kanye's mouth when he was purchasing mansions and thousand-dollar toddler tutus and, had there been some restraint and reserve shown at those moments, a GoFundMe account would not be necessary. Newsflash, asshole: I have a GoFundMe account, too and it's called a motherfucking job, and the sole contributor to said fund, no thanks to our governor's asinine and illegal pension contribution vetoes, is yours truly.

Yet another shining example of the rampant, reigning entitlement issues in our society was highlighted in a cry-baby style, woe is me essay written by some moronic millennial who penned an open letter to her employer at Yelp. She "didn't want to" have to work in an entry level position at entry level pay because, well, she just didn't want to. She was shattered over the fact that she'd spent the past year answering calls and talking to customers just for the hope that someday she'd be able to make memes and twitter jokes about food. Are you fucking kidding me?

I'm a little disappointed myself that, rather than chasing my dreams of being a professional writer who works from home, drinking Bloody Mary's on my lanai in Hawaii, I teach English. Guess what sweet-pea, making memes and Twitter jokes about food is a hobby, one for someone with intellect and humor, traits you obviously do not possess. Making money, on the other hand, is what happens when you work. At a job. While you're waiting for your dreams to come true. That's why adulthood is referred to as "the real world" as opposed to "the dream world."

I hate to rain on anyone's parade but, statistically speaking, most of us are not going to be rich, famous or powerful. We will not be rap stars, professional athletes, models, moguls and especially not famous YouTubers for God's sake. We will not live in mansions by the ocean, drive Bentleys down Hollywood Boulevard or have a spread in Forbes Magazine. We are not entitled to fortune and fame and all of that bullshit but, I truly believe, we are entitled to live and love and be happy.

Kanye and Yelp girl, and deadbeat dads alike, are likely not happy because they have failed to grow out of this ill-informed teenaged frame of mind, and who is to blame? An education system that socially promotes failing students. A probation system that does not enforce child support obligations. A societal construct wherein those who do are held to a higher standard of doing more, and those who don't are allowed to do so.   Diplomas become meaningless.   Court orders become unenforceable.   Hard work becomes obsolete. The notion that cheaters never win and winners never cheat becomes unquestioningly discredited.

If you haven't noticed, this has been pissing me off. A lot. But I'm working on that. I'm trying to be a better me, as the self-help books promote. I do feel strongly, though, that if I'm going to be a better me, you better be damned sure to be a better you. At least make an attempt to rise above your current level of slightly-better-than-complete-shit

A dear friend of mine encouraged me recently to rise above as well, when I had vented my frustrations regarding my ex's purposeful circumvention of a court order enforcing child support. I informed her that I did, in fact, intend to rise above him. In my car. As he crossed the street.

Then she asked me if I pray.
Uh oh. Now I know that I'm in trouble.
1. Because I don't pray and 2. Because someone thinks I need to.
Shit.

She went on to ask me if I have ever prayed for my ex's happiness. She's funny, right?   She was serious, though.   In case anyone requires further clarification pertaining to my feelings about my son's father, the answer was an emphatic, enthusiastic NO.

Well, that's not completely true. Sometimes I pray that he will drop dead, but that's probably not going to get me into the EZ Pass lane to heaven, so I'll just keep it simple. No, I don't pray.

While I'm not necessarily a proponent of prayer, I am an avid fan of literary devices and she kindly followed up her spiritual request with an analogy. She said that being angry is like swallowing poison and expecting the other person to die, a line referenced from time to time in AA programs. I think I've been drinking the poison for far too long now, so here comes the Hail Mary play.

I really don't want to be angry and resentful but, quite frankly, like Kanye to his money, I kind of feel entitled to my anger at this point, and that's difficult to let go of. It kind of reminds me of having a yard sale. You put all the shit you've spent years collecting out on your front lawn and then some asshole comes by and offers you fifty cents for it. The price you paid and the price they propose are incongruent and inequitable. But sometimes you have to clean house.

What pushed me to the brink of a homicidal rage, if you care to know, was ten dollars. Seriously, it was ten fucking dollars. After receiving a court order a few weeks back enforcing my ex to pay off some of the tens of thousands of dollars he owes in child support, he decided to see my court order and raise me one big fuck you. Rather than abiding by, you know, the law, he shorted me ten bucks that week. Just to be a dick, I presume.

In any event, I decided to heed my friend's advice and take a shot at the whole being full of grace and praying thing. Of course, I decided it would be best to start tomorrow. Well, that particular tomorrow

I found myself in a foxhole prayer situation. While I was preoccupied and supremely pissed about my ten dollars, I was bitch-slapped across the face with a legitimate reason for prayer.

That day, my other half – the better one, by the way, was involved in a four car crash on the highway. Everyone was alright, thank God, but cars were totaled, traffic delayed and nerves shot. Fire in the hole.

That night, I prayed.
I prayed for everything and everyone I am so fortunate to have in my life.
I prayed for family and friends.
I prayed for forgiveness.
I prayed because I was thankful.

A very long time ago, someone told me that if everyone in the world placed their troubles in a bag, when it's your turn to choose, you better hope you pick out your own. I would choose my own. Not just because I am equipped and accustomed to coping with them, but because things can always be worse.

I am thankful to have been reminded of what is important, what is relevant and what it's really all about. Life is about playing your hand, however shitty it may be, and beating the odds. It's about starting at the bottom and moving up because, after all, the only way to get out of a hole is to climb. We can't resign ourselves to remain in our foxholes paralyzed by fear and bitterness, eventually we must climb out, hit the ground running, and engage in the battle for our own happiness, with faith and hope by our side. Never say never. Never say I don't want to. Never say I can't.

So, here goes nothing.

God, grant me the serenity to accept the things I cannot change, courage to change the things I can, and wisdom to know the difference.

9: Bloody Mary (land)

Suggested pairing: Bloody Mary

This particular beverage recipe is my very own and one of my shining achievements in life. It has evolved through trial and error, and taste test after delicious taste test.

2 ounces vodka   *Spicy V8 Vegetable Juice*

1 tablespoon spicy horseradish   *½ teaspoon celery salt*

2 tablespoons Lea and Perrins Worcestershire Sauce

Lemon wedge, squeezed

Fill pint glass with ice and add vodka. Pour in vegetable juice leaving ½ inch at top and add remaining ingredients. Shake until chilled and combined. Garnish the shit out of this with celery, blue cheese stuffed olives, shrimp, bacon or whatever else makes you bloody happy.

Cheers.

Baltimore, Maryland. Home to the Orioles, the Ravens and, on this particular alcohol induced drama, a bird of a different, fucked up feather. Unlike the fantasy business trip to Virginia, this excursion did, in fact, take place, and also took his addiction to a whole new, extraordinary level of absurdity.

I don't recall the timeframe of this outing, most likely because I have blocked out a significant sum of his bullshit, nor do I recall the purpose of it, assuming there actually was one. I do, however, distinctly recollect the fact that the drunken bird did not fly solo. He was travelling with a coworker, and he was supposedly travelling sober.

Pay no attention to the bottles hidden in the garage. Avert your eyes from the staggering, your ears from the slurring, and your nose from the rancid scent of whiskey sweat. Disregard the poorly forged AA meeting attendance logs and mounting debt. Of course, he is not drinking, because he says he's not.

At this stage in the game, I'd had ample time and experience to hone my strategy and skill at drunken chess. I had learned to anticipate his movements and react with patience, precision and purpose. It became an exercise in mental manipulation and psychological stamina. Sadly, despite my polished skillset, my key role in his game had been demoted from Queen to Pawn, a vital team member once able to move any direction and defended at all costs, now used, manipulated and sacrificed to gain advantage on the board.

The saga began in the wee hours of a Wednesday morning in June, about 6 years ago. This epic fuck-up was brought to my attention via text message, his most preferred form of lack of communication. I like to refer to these messages as "untimely."

They come at off hours, during periods of compounding stress, and as an addendum to the scroll of various other inopportune memoranda regarding various degrees of what one would deem rock bottom, but never was.

We have a long-running witticism in our family regarding the dreaded untimely death of a pet. Never ones to pass up irony, or a "too soon" joke, we enjoy the banter pertaining to the loss of a furry friend. Despite the growing graveyard of household cats and dogs, my parents and I continue to invest in all things adorable.

These bundles of mammalian joy enhance the home, contributing years of companionship and sometimes over the top spoonage to our otherwise redundant existence. The problem with this pet formula is, as my brothers humorously point out, there is an inevitable expiration date attached to these additions. Hence the untimely death predicament.

The irony of the untimeliness of eventual death, as well as the untimeliness of the text messages, is that there is no good time for dying or for being a dick. No one looks at a calendar, draws a big red circle around a date in the near future, and says "yeah, three weeks from Thursday looks like it would work to hit up the euthanasia clinic." I never awoke bright-eyed and bushy-tailed, all my shit together thinking, "nothing scheduled, today would totally work for me to field some bullshit." This particular Wednesday in June most certainly was not that day.

Taking into consideration how frequent these messages had become, one would think I would be better equipped to handle them, or at least anticipate them. No, sir. The hits keep coming and it never really gets easier to predict the punch.

1 New Text Message.

"I'm in the hospital. Almost a broken jaw."

Laugh or cry – dealer's choice.

Memory Full.

Incoming Text Message.

Fucking flip phone for having no memory. Fucking Type B personality for hoarding messages.

Scrolling to locate messages acceptable for deletion, was just the jolly trip down memory lane required to properly handle that morning's state of affairs. Good times! I had the brief opportunity to revisit a selection of his prior cringe-worthy communications before anteing up to this one. Crashed the car. Not coming home for dinner. Missed his flight. Lost his wallet. Lost his job.

1 New Text Message.

"Not almost. Jaw is broken."

In an effort to expedite you through this super-fun process, I will spare you the details of the three phone calls to my husband wherein he asserted his continued sobriety with conviction, while simultaneously throwing himself a little pity party. Evidently, upon exiting an Orioles game, he was separated from his co-worker and mugged by hooligans while minding his very sober and upstanding citizen business, on his way back to the hotel. Poor soul.

What to do, what to do? I sat quietly, with my coffee and cigarette in trembling hands, and attempted to focus. I revisited the facts, and I use that term loosely, of the situation.

1. He was in Baltimore on business.
2. He was at a baseball game.
3. He was separated from his friend.
4. He was mugged.
5. He was in the hospital.
6. He was sober.

Timeout. He was mugged? I was only aware of this "fact" because he had kindly sent the untimely text message to inform me as such. The untimely text just got a little more-timely, it seems.

He texted me. He spoke with me, albeit garbled and through a broken jaw. He contacted me. On his phone. After being mugged. Now, I'm not an expert in the art of alleyway assaults and sidewalk stealing, but why would someone take the time to comprehensively shatter your face, rendering you incapacitated, and not steal your shit? My limited knowledge of the inner workings of the inner city of Baltimore, is that if you get mugged, they're going to take everything including your underwear if it's not too dirty. And yet he had his phone. He took the beating like a champion and defended his phone until the end, just so that he may keep me upraised of such events. What a guy.

Upon further investigation, I also found that he had managed to maintain ownership over his wallet, credit cards and all of his cash. Well, isn't he amazing? He must be the Batman of Baltimore, the Magneto of Maryland. Literally unbelievable.

Being that my private investigating expertise had become as finely tuned as my chess game, I began to do some probing. First order of business was to contact his friend from whom he became disconnected. I located his name and cell phone number on a contact sheet my ex had in a pile of papers on his desk at home. I called him. At 7:40am. And I was not friendly.

I introduced myself and asked him what the fuck had gone on the night before, in that order and in that manner. I could almost hear the squeaky wheel in his brain turning, with the hungover hamster flopping around inside. He was grasping at straws, attempting to piece together the prior night's events, while drunkenly struggling to protect his fucked up friend from the wrath of his seemingly insane wife.

Evidently, this man was separated from my ex after an Orioles game, and was subsequently mugged on his way back to the hotel. Well, I'll be. The stars had aligned and the same exact thing had happened to him! I called my husband back, armed with some deadly ammunition.

"I'm going to ask you one more time if you were drinking last night and, be advised before you answer, that I just got off the phone with your idiot co-worker."

"Ok, I was drinking."

Check. I had now managed to outsmart him in his chess game. Sadly, I would not remain ahead for long. I had to plan my next move. At this juncture, I had the King in check but my own anxiety began to cloud my thinking, forcing me to execute poorly and move chaotically.

I still, to this very day, regret my next move.

I printed directions to Mercy Medical Center. I dropped my son off at my parents. I drove to Maryland to pick him up. I should have left him there. I should have left him there until. Until he figured it out on his own. Until he sobered up and realized what he had done. Until he hit bottom.

I drove for close to four hours in traffic to get there. When I arrived, the nurses kindly directed me to his room and gave me the condescending "there, there" look, as they sympathized with his pain and suffering. Poor him. Nobody gave a fuck about my pain and suffering, I'll tell you that, and they definitely didn't take to kindly to me commanding him to get his shit and get in the car, while failing to acknowledge the extent of his injuries.

I did not care about his broken jaw, as no one cared about my broken spirit. Truth be told, I wanted to give him a broken nose to go with it. I still don't know what actually transpired in Baltimore that night, and maybe he doesn't either.

We drove for hours in silence. We picked up a prescription for painkillers. None for me by the way. We picked up my son. We went back to the same cycle of bullshit, the same game of chess that had been rigged against me for so long. Then, at his request, we went to the diner to get him a smoothie.

Since his jaw was to be wired shut for the next six to eight weeks, he was unable to speak, or eat, or brush his teeth. All he could do now....was drink.
Checkmate.
Shit.

10: Manhattan

Suggested pairing: Rye Manhattan

When you stay up all night drinking in the city that never sleeps.

2 ounces Rye Whiskey

2 tablespoons sweet vermouth

Dash of Angostura Bitters

Cherry

Combine rye, vermouth and bitters in an ice-filled glass. Stir until very chilled. Strain into martini glass. Garnish with cherry.

Cheers.

Often, the most difficult aspect of a night out on the town is the logistics, which become increasingly cringe-worthy as the drinking becomes increasingly binge-worthy. What begins as a simple trip from point A to point B can rapidly spiral into a web of deception and destruction. In rare cases and, depending upon the individual, these circumstances may result in a phenomenal family folktale or a footnote in a long line of fuck-ups.

Always a fan of brevity, I deeply appreciate the wisdom of Charlie Chaplin, a man made famous for his soundless and profound contribution to silent film. He expressed himself mainly through action and behavior but, on a rare and wonderful occasion, he imparted his insight on the world through words. He was typically short and sweet, and to the point, and he was usually right. Sir Charles Spencer, as he was formally known, once said that "a man's true character comes out when he's drunk." Well, isn't that the truth.

We are all characters in the film of life. Some are kind and generous, some are exuberant and entertaining. Some are subtle and sweet, while others are bold and brazen. Our character, the core of who we are as human beings, can be clearly visible and advertised in an "as is" fashion, or it may be indelibly guarded and shrouded in fine print. In either case, this character, this internal modus operandi is sure to rear its head, however ugly, when plied with alcohol.

My brother is an excellent individual. Insanely intelligent and wickedly funny, his character is one that would contribute depth and humanity to anyone's life story. His part in my life has been one of friend, family and funny-man, and his walk-on role in others' carries with it the wit and wherewithal to propel a scene to comic success. He has a skill for sarcasm and talent for "too soon," as well as an innate ability to allow the world to right itself around him. He is always in good spirits and, when drinking them, his humor and intellect are highlighted.

Years back, at the tail end of an epic guy's weekend in Atlanta, this character performed an Oscar-worthy comedic stunt, one that was to be conceptualized in insanity, executed in intoxication and to live in infamy. Both of my brothers, and a handful of their friends, were closing out an all-night whiskey marathon when they determined that they required some sober assistance in arriving home safely. While they frequently operated on auto-pilot when traversing the city on foot, they had ventured too far from home to perform as pedestrians.

Both broskie's traits were on display in Technicolor that night. The older, ever economically and environmentally responsible, furnished funds to the driver for his share of the ride and, after exiting the vehicle, proceeded to take out the garbage and recycling, however shitfaced he may have been. Never straying from his true character, he managed to crusade through the cocktails performing mathematical operations and equations to determine tab and tip, and further overcoming his intoxication in order to complete his daily chores while simultaneously giving a nod and wink to Mother Earth. Bravo, bro!

Ahhhh, the youngest of the siblings three. The epitome of a survivor of youngest child syndrome, one to whom the rules do not apply and who does not apply the rules. What he lacks compared to us in life experience, he surely makes up for with lively experiences. Somehow, despite every effort otherwise, the world around him always rights itself in his favor, this event proving no exception to his rule.

Following in our other brother's footsteps, he contemplated his contribution to the cabbie and exited the car. He navigated himself up the stairs to the residence and proceeded inside to procure payment for services rendered. While searching the premises for appropriate means of imbursement, the remaining intoxicated individuals attempted to depart from the driver's car, but did so leaving a cell phone behind in the back seat, in addition to an unwanted gratuity of vomit.

Finally, after substantial consideration on the part of my brother and frustration on the part of the cabbie, he returned with the only obvious form of compensation suitable for this shitshow: blankets. Yes, he paid with blankets. Never mind the jar of change in the bedroom or credit cards in the wallet. Never mind the fact that quilts have almost no monetary value in the transportation industry. Never mind the obvious absurdity of such a notion, he paid with blankets.

Had it not been for the convenient leave behind of barf and belongings, this astonishing feat may have been forgotten in the blackout state where it had been achieved. Thank heavens for his friend heaving. When they called the abandoned phone the next day, the driver answered and agreed to return the phone, and the blankets. They were all equally pleased about the phone, but overwhelmingly perplexed about the blankets.

The driver returned and recounted the events leading up to that moment: the fare, the phone, the barfing, and the bedding. My brother apologized profusely, compensated him generously and then laughed hysterically, as we have for years since. All travel and transportation costs are, in one way or another, measured in an estimate of blankets to this very day.

We can laugh at this story because, true to his character, my brother's comedic genius shone through in a situation that was nothing short of ridiculous. There was no malicious intent, in fact, there was likely no intent at all. He just did the best he could with the terrible tools he had at that moment, albeit blankets and blackout, and the conflict was resolved similar to that of a thirty-minute sit-com. There was laughter, tears, a little puke, and a lesson learned in the end: you can't pay for a cab with a blanket, unless you're my brother.

Just as Keanu Reeves would have ruined the role of Hannibal Lecter and shitted up The Silence of the Lambs, not all characters can perform a particular role or carry a certain scene. My ex attempted a similar stunt on his way home from NYC several years ago, and the resounding review was the equivalent of a truck load of rotten tomatoes. While the plot was eerily similar and the setting was comparable, the character was undeveloped and the backstory was just plain bad.

His business trips, which can more accurately be described as none of my business trips, usually initiated innocently enough, and quickly descended into a compilation of strip clubs, bar fights and public intoxication. Throughout the course of this downward spiral, his affable veneer melted away and his belligerence and bullshit quickly rose to the surface. By evening's end, all that remained was the core of his character, the dark monster that was ruled by alcohol and riddled with insecurity. The monster reared its ugly head that night, trust and believe.

Evidently, his meetings had run late, you know, late into the night as real business meetings tend to do, and he'd missed all available trains running out of the city for the day. Adding insult to injury, his phone had also died and someone had water-boarded him with vodka. Pour soul. I'm not sure of the exact time that he finally stumbled in, but I can tell you it was half past me wanting a divorce, and a quarter to him wetting the bed.

I didn't realize he'd arrived at the house because, at this stage in our dysfunction, I was sleeping in a separate bedroom and, in all honesty, was kind of hoping he wouldn't come back. I was unaware that he was passed out in the next room until I called his cell phone, once again, in an attempt to verify either his estimated time of arrival or his time of death, I was never sure which one it would be. The voice on the other end of the line was unfamiliar, angry and carried a heavy accent.

He informed me that he had driven my ex from the eastern side of Manhattan to our home on the western side of New Jersey. He also explained that his drunken passenger had passed out in the back of the car and, upon arrival at his destination, became argumentative and refused to pay for the ride. The man vented his frustrations regarding long hours, low pay and belligerent customers, and then verbally sucker punched me when he broke down into tears and expounded upon the amount he works to support his growing family.

I empathized with him on the ways in which we bust our asses to support our children, only to have our dedication derailed by a delinquent. I assured him he would receive his hard-earned money in addition to a well-deserved apology. The call ended, and so did an exceptionally shitty day.

When my ex came to the next morning, I instructed him to get dressed and get in the car. He was confused and indignant, a combination that I was all too familiar with, when he inquired as to where we would be going. I told him we were going to New York so that he could pay his driver for the services he declined to pay for the evening prior. He said no.

He actually said no.
He essentially blamed the driver for trying to screw him out of money, and said no. That was only until I told him that the driver had his phone. Then he said yes.

So, off we went. The walk, or drive in this case, of shame.
I drove him to the city, not to retrieve his property or even his dignity, but to pay the cab fare he should have paid the night before, the same fare he refused to pay that morning. I drove him to the city to do what was fair and, in this instance, the fare was fair.

The striking fundamental difference between the story of my brother and the story of my ex is the function of their behavior. However asinine and ill-informed as my brother's duvet cover currency may have been, it was an attempt to do the right thing. He wanted to pay his share of the fare and, despite his intentions being good, his execution was, well, not. His true character was shown while he was drunk. He scrambled, searched the apartment and came up with the only means of payment he could muster at the time. Yes, it was a blanket, but it was an attempt nonetheless.

My ex, conversely, made every attempt to withhold payment from the cabbie. He denied any wrongdoing and made every effort imaginable to skirt responsibility. He did this until it negatively impacted him and, only then, did he concede to doing the right thing.

It is evident that our true character is exposed when we are drunk, but it is defined when we are sober. It is defined by the ways in which we treat others and the manner in which we overcome adversity. It is defined by how we accept responsibility for our mistakes and express humility for our accomplishments. Character is who we are when we are alone or in the company of others, when we are at rock bottom or the pinnacle of success, when we are drunk or sober.

Character is what makes the beds we have to lie in, and we can either accept blankets or bullshit to keep us company. I prefer to go to bed knowing that I have done the best that I can do with what I have, confident that I do the right thing, whatever that may be. I don't like to brag but, I sleep pretty well at night and, p.s. I don't wet the fucking bed.

11: Chaser

Suggested pairing: Pickleback Shot

This right here is some funky shit but, believe it or not, it goes down smooth.

Jameson

Pickle Juice

Pour Jameson in one shot glass and pickle juice in another. Chase whiskey with brine. Enjoy?

Cheers.

For what I lack in the brown liquor drinking department, my brothers surely compensate. They are notorious for imbibing in this renowned Irish concoction, and while I am unable and unwilling to partake, they do make it look like fun. Their alcohol abilities come equipped with near superhero strength during the night and enviable auto-pilot ability following. Mine, however, are short-lived and short-sighted, rivaling only a dud firework that displays an initial burst of light, only to fizzle out and wind up on the ground.

One evening, a few years back, I accompanied my youngest brother and a friend to a local bar for some happy hour spirits and snacks. It was that night that I encountered a drink that, in all of my bartending experience, had somehow eluded me. The Pickleback. Now, I'm not sure if he acquired this particular alcoholic anomaly via a stint in the south, or through sheer liquor genius, but he was an ardent advocate and a cultivated connoisseur.

Also known as the Piskey Whickle or the Bartender's Handshake, this particular shot rose to fame in the mid-2000s in, of all places, Brooklyn, NY. Evidently, a rough-riding, rough around the edges bar patron requested a shot of whiskey and a chaser of pickle juice, and so the dream was born. The term was coined and it became a phenomenon in bars across the country. Not only does the drink have curb appeal as a unique conversation starter, it additionally provides a scientifically supported cure for the common hangover. Brine for the belly and hair of the dog, according to researchers, provide the magical medicine for the Whiskey Flu.

Sometimes a chaser is necessary, in order to swallow something that is unpleasant or even vomit-inducing. Sometimes it is essential in curing the destructive after-effects of our own drinking, or for intervening in the during-effects of someone else's. Sometimes a chaser is a last resort and, when that is the case, it can be the smartest fucking decision you will ever make.

Much like the brief history of the Pickleback shot, my ex's relapse into alcoholism came seemingly out of nowhere following a decade of successful sobriety. The Bartender's Handshake erupted into popularity suddenly and without notice, much like a certain individual's affinity for alcohol came rebounding back with massive momentum and fucked up force. His reversion was riddled with bingeing and belligerence, harassment and hazardous driving, rehabs and restraining orders, DUI's and downright douchiness. Due to the residual bad taste resulting from his many stupendously idiotic, dangerous and self-destructive decisions, a chaser was definitely in order.

March 2013. The top of the bottoms with regard to his addiction. For someone who never manages to actually reach bottom, he sure has a knack for digging deeper.

At this juncture in the perpetual downward spiral, The Division of Youth and Family Services was in the process of closing our case. Oh, did I forget to mention the infinite joys of having the family division involved in our lives? What a wondrous experience. Since my ex, during his passing, unsupervised parenting period, had made the ultimate asshole decision to drive our son to school (pre-school by the way) drunk from the night before, DYFS had become involved.

I have fairly extensive experience with this agency because of my work in school systems. I have made many calls and filed reports, and dealt with a variety of representatives and advocates. I am in no way denigrating the work that they do. They are exceptionally overextended and equally understaffed. I will say, however, having to invite them into my own personal affairs was a completely different ballgame, one that calls for many whiskeys and many chasers.

The concept of DYFS is like Communism – great idea on paper but, when executed, is not at all as fair as one would anticipate. Because a certain individual was a drunk and a liar and repeatedly placed our son in harm's way, protocol was to conduct supervised visitation and home visits. Agreed – totally a smart move. Oh wait, you need to visit my home, too? Weekly? And take notes? And look at my shit? And quietly pass judgements on me for not doing anything wrong? Super. I'm in.

While this was wholly uncomfortably and invasive, I complied because A.) I had nothing to hide, and B.) It protected my son from what his father was hiding.

It was bullshit – I'm not going to lie. It is extremely creepy and weird to have some random 23-year-old single girl, with a newly attained college degree and a cheap pant-suit from Marshalls, exploring your home, with the fate of your family in her nicely manicured hands. I've had students that were older than this chick. I've had more experience than this chick. But I smiled and nodded and kept it moving because, although I was the one being observed, I was not the one being watched.

I was the one that called them in. I asked for this in an effort to protect my little boy. I would deal with whatever discomfort and distress this would cause me because, after all, it's not about me. Sadly, despite the obvious alcohol abuse and evident need for continued intervention, the agency prepared to close their case after several months and leave it in the hands of another agency to continue supervised visitations. This was the whiskey shot that put me over the edge.

Next comes the chaser.

I'm not sure if I should be proud or ashamed, but luckily my very best friend had a recommendation for a private investigator she had used in her own fucked up custody conflict. Hooray for friends! I contacted said investigator and, true to PI form, established a contractual agreement which would eventually lead to a small sting operation. We never met. We communicated via email and exchanged paperwork and pertinent information by way of a PO Box. We only spoke once, but that comes later.

The necessity to hire a literal "chaser" stemmed from the fact, and I mean fact, that I was fully aware that my ex was still drinking heavily, in spite of every assurance otherwise. I could not, in good conscience, allow my son to be placed in a potentially dangerous situation. I would not allow it. And so begins the chase.

This chase was harsh like the pickle juice. Even though it soothes the sting of the initial whiskey shot, it still maintains a bitterness in its own right. It is disgusting but necessary, especially for someone who loathes brown liquor. It did the trick. It all went down like this.

I sent the PI a photograph of my ex, the make and model of his car, his work schedule, and a potential day and time that heavy drinking may ensue. Sherlock Holmes shit, right? I'm no dummy. If I've gained anything from this decidedly destructive experience it's that I know the signs and I know how to follow them. Alcoholics may be erratic but they are ironically predictable. It was almost too easy.

The detective solicited a female associate of his to conduct the investigation. She waited in a parked car outside his work, nearing the end of his shift. When he left, she chased. He went directly to a bar, and went in with bells on. The bartender knew him by name and was especially pleased when he entered bearing gifts from his own place of employment. A little midnight snack for the bartender will surely get you good service! I guess he's no dummy either.

He proceeded to down 4 double vodka and tonics in one hour and five minutes. I think it's pretty safe to say that 8 shots in an hour will get you good and fucked up. I'm no expert but, vodka is alcohol, right? That's an odd beverage selection for someone who is actively attending AA meetings and abstaining from drinking. Maybe he should have ordered a chaser as well.

The real kick in the balls here is that, after throwing back enough booze to make a small horse drunk, he drove home. Yep – hopped right in his car, 2 DUI's and an abundance of arrogance in tow. That fucker drove home. This is what he deems honest and appropriate behavior. This is what he pretends to believe is good enough for our son. What the fuck.

The next morning, a Saturday, I received my first and only call from the private investigator. He provided me with the disturbing details of my ex's behavior and relayed the ease with which he obtained this information. He emailed me photographs of him at the bar. And a video. His binge gave me a hangover.

In the days that followed, I refused visitation between him and my son. No shit, Sherlock. Pun intended. There was an obvious safety risk – not that I didn't know before, but now I had proof from the chaser. He responded to my refusal with the obvious addict rebuttal – deflection and provocation. He sent text messages and emails at a constant and alarming pace. They came at all hours of the day and night, each one more hurtful and harassing than the last.

He degraded me.
He insulted me.
He called me names. Every disgusting name you could possibly imagine and some you can't.
He just.
Wouldn't.
Stop.

I checked doors and windows to make sure they were locked. I checked, and I rechecked. I sat and stared and cried. And didn't sleep.

I called my attorney.
I called the police.
I testified in front of a judge in a closed court.
I was granted a temporary restraining order.
But enough about me....
He violated the restraining order.
He was arrested.

He went to jail.
He went to rehab.
It didn't work. Again.

Without the chaser, Pickleback or PI, I would be in constant fear for my son's safety. So, while he's chasing down his demons, he can't chase me. Thank God for that because, while I will always have to chase down the truth, I will never have to throw back another nasty shot of his crazy.

12: Shaken

Suggested pairing: 007 Martini

My word is my bond, James Bond.

2 ounces vodka

½ ounce dry vermouth

Twist of Lemon

Fill cocktail shaker with ice. Pour ingredients over ice and shake the shit out of it until thoroughly chilled. Strain into martini glass. Garnish with lemon twist.

Cheers.

Don't you love a good old fashioned risk assessment? I'm sorry, are you unfamiliar with that term? Of course you are, because you are a normal human being whose life never skyrockets to a stratospheric level of crazy. Let me school you on this particular incident of insanity.

A risk assessment, in its simplest form, is a collection of clinical data utilized in an effort to calculate and predict potential safety hazards, based upon an individual's psychological temperament as well as their behavior history. Sounds fun, right?

The evaluation is comprised of a battery of psychological inventory exams and interviews, as well as an extensive appraisal of various submissions including, but not limited to court orders, arrest records, DYFS reports and alcoholic rehabilitation program attendance. Well then. Logic would dictate that if one does, in fact, have these particular documents available for review, a significant problem already exists. But, just to be certain, let's do some psych evals for shits and giggles. Better safe than sorry.

I don't know about you, but I've done some fucked up shit in my life. I've made more than one astoundingly stupid mistake and paid for them in the past, but I have never, ever, put my son's physical or emotional well-being in jeopardy. Based on those statistics, my son is batting .500 in the responsible parent department, and he deserves better than that. Way better.

We all have issues. I have anxiety. Sporadic episodes resulting in panic attacks, and more frequent events surrounding social circumstances. I loathe large gatherings of people and forced small talk. On occasion, I have been known to erupt into a full blown panic attack, complete with heart palpitations and hyperventilation. Good times. But I take a Klonopin, and I digress.

Had I been the subject of said risk assessment, I can say with certainty that the evaluation would reveal my anxious tendencies. It may reflect some level of social maladjustment and discomfort, but I am sure it would not peg me as a narcissist or a sociopath or a serial killer in the making. The tests are eerily accurate, as though the administrator of the exam has crawled down the rabbit hole into the wonderland of the mind, gaining unadulterated access to the inner workings of the psyche. Scary shit.

But the test itself proves to be far less frightening than the results. I know my ex-husband – better than most people do, probably better than he even knows himself. Despite his outbursts and flair for the disturbing, he is rather transparent. His cycle of addiction is like a short film on repeat. The actors and the set may evolve from time to time, but the plot remains fairly constant.

The purpose of this evaluation was to determine possible risk to my son if he were to be parented by his father in an unsupervised setting. At the time that this interview was conducted, my son was visiting with his father for one hour, every other week, at an agency that facilitated safe and healthy interactions in a clinical location.

My son was 6 years old then, and had already sustained a sadly significant quantity of psychological and emotional damage at the hands of his father. The entire year leading up to the risk assessment was a shit show. My ex had been arrested for yet another DUI and had done three consecutive stints in rehab facilities, to no avail. Additionally, I had secured a Final Restraining Order resulting from his continued harassment and degradation fueled by heavy alcohol use abuse. His participation in my son's life had diminished to little more than a bi-weekly Happy Meal coinciding with an unhappy visit.

The restraining order granted me, not only a much needed permanent vacation from his barrage of insults and nastygram assaults but, more importantly, sole custody of our son. The order also indicated the necessity for a risk assessment to be completed so that we may eventually work toward his father playing a more active role in my son's life. That is the goal, after all, right?

Throughout the domestic violence trial, his attorney paraded his sobriety around like a blue ribbon pony at a fair. There were letters from therapists, certificates from rehabilitation facilities, testimonies from family members. It was nauseating. I was accused of intentionally withholding our son for my own selfish purposes and failing to acknowledge or believe his newfound sobriety. I was the bad guy? Really?

In any event, the judge ruled with compassion and conviction and granted my request. Ten days after the ruling he was arrested for his 4th DUI.

Although the restraining order mandated a risk assessment be completed as soon as possible, he failed to initiate the process, either as a result of ignorance or indolence - complacency being a consistent quality displayed in all aspects of his addiction.

Sometime later, my ex again began demanding more time, unsupervised time, with our son. Reluctant and with obvious reservations, I researched the risk assessment process and located a qualified individual to perform the interview.

The court approved psychotherapist agreed to work with our family, begin therapy with our son and complete the assessment. Let's view the highlights reel, shall we? I declare a drinking game of Risk! If you sense something risky, take a shot.

One Hour Clinical Interview Summary:

He admits to "alcoholism and 3 stays at alcohol rehabilitation facilities in 2013."

He admits that he "lost his driver's license 2 times while married."

He admits to "driving while intoxicated as he drove his son."

He claims to "have remained sober since August 22, 2013."

32 Page Parenting History Survey:

He states, "I have a drinking problem so my son's mother is concerned for his safety."

He claims his "ex-wife is withholding access to our child."

He admits that "I have a lied about recovery in the past."

He refers to "severe hostility between himself and his ex-wife."

He requests "for visitation to go back to original divorce agreement."

Test Results from MMPI-2, a 567 item true false scale designed to assess social and personal maladjustment:

His profile is "most akin to individuals who experience chronic psychological maladjustment most likely characterized by impulsivity and compulsive behavior."

He tends to "manipulate others in mostly passive-aggressive ways."

Individuals like this "tend to leave treatment without significantly changing behavior, making problems likely to recur."

He "presented some clear personality problems that are pertinent to an assessment to his day-to-day functioning as a parent."

He "has a tendency to engage in irresponsible, immature and possibly antisocial behavior."

"His impulsivity, low frustration tolerance and need for immediate self-gratification influence his functioning as a parent."

He tends to be "somewhat self-centered and those with his profile are difficult to positively influence."

Have a glass of water or go pull the trigger and we'll continue.

Test Results from the MCMI-3, a 175 item true false scale designed to assess emotional and interpersonal difficulties:

"His relationships seem to be shallow and fleeting and may be characterized by his manipulative deceptions."

He may be "typically unable to delay gratification and often acts on impulses with insufficient deliberation and poor judgement."

He has "a tendency to be untrustworthy and unreliable."

He may "intentionally or carelessly fail to meet marital, parental, employment or financial obligations."

"His defiant and resentful acts are fused with self-destructive behaviors."

"Temper outbursts may be intense and unanticipated violence may be expressed."

It's all good, if you throw up some of the booze, you'll have room for more.

Summary and Opinion:
My son is "at risk being unsupervised" in his father's presence.

Data indicates that "he is untrustworthy, tends to cooperate only when being directly observed and only values his opinions."
It is further recommended that "visitation is supervised."
Also, "prior to visits, he is to perform an alcohol swab test."
"Therapeutic father-son sessions are to last for one additional year once driver's license is restored."

Further recommendations included an updated risk assessment and substance abuse evaluation, continued swab testing, proof of consistent employment and proof of AA involvement. The game of Risk is a board-game of world domination where, in order to win, you must attack to acquire territory and defend to keep it from your opponents. I hate board games and I especially hate this one.
I do not wish to control all of the territory. I do not wish to engage with a combative opponent, but such is the game of Risk and here we are. Fortunately, after engaging in a decade long bout of this stupid pastime, I have learned a thing or two about strategy.

I protect my pieces, namely my son, but also my dignity and my sanity. I control the board, by default, but I control the board. I will not allow an unworthy opponent to infringe on my territory or to invade my space. I do not risk the safety of my pieces. I dominate, maybe not the world, but I dominate.

Engaging in a sport with an alcoholic is always a game of Risk. Because it is not a game restricted to two players, there is always more than one loser. While I maintain control of the board in one way or another, I by no means consider myself a winner. I lose, my son loses and, in his own sick and demented way, my ex loses as well.

The game will make you dizzy, disoriented and debilitated, and leave you shaken to the core. At this point, I would like to respectfully withdraw from another round of drinks and games. At the risk of sounding like a lightweight, cash me out.

13: Cut Off

Suggested pairing: Nothing.

You're cut off, now get the fuck out of here.

Cheers.

I don't enjoy the word cunt. My vocabulary is vast and colorful but even I have my limits. I love fuck and motherfucker and a sweet combo like God dammit sonofabitch, but cunt has a distasteful quality to it, rivaled only by moist and panties which, when uniting all three results in an unfathomable abomination to the English language.

Somehow, by the grace of the gods of tenure, I have maintained a semi-functional filter at work and have managed to avoid dropping the f-bomb on my puberty-stricken angels. There have been a handful of occasions when I came close, making a last second switch from fuck to fine, and countless times I've really wanted to vomit inappropriate vernacular but, shout out to the baby Jesus, I've resisted the undeniable temptation to call those motherfuckers, well, motherfuckers.

There's absolutely nada the matter with adult language. It's fun. It's versatile. It's all-around fucktastic. That being said, there is not only a time and a place, but a right way and a wrong way to employ such lingo.

Calling the mother of your child a cunt is the wrong fucking way to use that word. There is no time to call the mother of your child a cunt. Not when she's run up your credit card, or locked the keys in the car, or even when she's called you an asshole, which you obviously are if you then call her a cunt. There is no place to call her a cunt, either. Don't call your baby's mama a cunt on the phone, via email or to her face.

Think of the word cunt, with regard to the mother of your child, like green eggs and ham. Do not do it here or there, do not do it anywhere.

Just don't. Don't call a woman a cunt. Especially, ESPECIALLY, when your child has resided in her body and violently exited her lady parts. If you do, you, my friend are a fucking cunt.

As hideous as the term cunt is, the fallout of divorce can be relatively just as ugly. Let's face it, once you have determined that you no longer wish to be married to your spouse, there is an almost immediate shift from love to hate, and shit gets nasty tout de suite. While there are amicable dissolutions that exist wherein two people lovingly agree to pull a Paltrow and consciously uncouple, the vast majority of people divorce because they can't fucking stand each other any longer.

Now comes the down and dirty. A friend of mine once told me that a family court judge had, in an effort to explain the bitterness of divorce, referred to those going through the process in court as good people behaving badly. No shit. Apparently, as the shiny golden ring slips off, so does the mask of social grace, mutual respect and all-around acceptable behavior. Divorce court becomes a circus of sorts, featuring caged animals hungry for human flesh and begrudgingly performing ridiculous stunts in an effort to impress the audience. The judge is the ringmaster, the attorneys the lion tamers, and the husband and wife devolve into primitive versions of their former selves, strutting and smirking in their Sunday best while, at the same time, a fraction of a second away from attacking anything that moves.

So what makes people behave like animals? Like cunts?

It's all about the Benjamins, baby. Shortly after my thirtieth birthday, and right around the time my ex started banging the manager at his country club, shit hit the fan. We had formulated a half-baked, crackpot idea to share the house while no longer sharing our lives and, oddly enough, it worked for a while. Here's how it jived, in case you're looking for pointers, which I sincerely hope you are not because you've come to the wrong place.

I stayed at the house during the week with our son while my soon-to-be ex-husband worked, and slept at his parents' house. On the weekends, he would stay at our marital residence to care for our son and I would bartend, then stay at a friend's house at night. Seems legit, right? It was all good in the hood until he got busted in bed with golf girl by his parents' housekeeper, and realized that it would be age-appropriate for him to acquire his own private residence. And so he did.

I actually took him house hunting to procure an apartment. I had to because he, again, had lost his license, but I digress. I admit this was an unusual approach, one that I would not likely reattempt, but it worked for the time being and so, a bachelor pad was born.
Life went on for the next few months, and we went on with our lives separately and accordingly. He with his hole in one, and I with my son. Then things went all south and cunty.

Since we were operating in an unorthodox, off the books manner, there was no set agreement as to how certain financial obligations would be addressed outside of a verbal, bullshit promise to take care of business. I admit, I was naïve. Looking back, I wonder how I could have been so stupid but I was young and inexperienced in the world of adulting and divorcing. That's the thing about this process: you don't get it until you got it and, sometimes, you get it a little too late.

As months passed and the realization of being a separated, single mother began to set in, I was bitch-slapped with the harsh reality that I was going to have to do a lot of shit I had never done before. My ex's presence was ever so gradually fading from the forefront, and I became the head of household, a position for which I was overwhelmingly underqualified.

But I'm a resilient cunt, so I put on my big girl panties and got going. I mowed the lawn. I sanded and painted wood and shit. I took out the garbage, got the oil changed in the car and frequented Home Depot. I was virtually unstoppable.

In addition to all of my patriarchal pedantry, I also took it upon myself to delve into the financial responsibilities of the home. Up until this point, I had never filed my own taxes or paid the mortgage or managed the utilities. I contributed money but had not managed any of the bills myself – he had always assumed that role. Yes, I am aware of how pathetically juvenile that sounds. I was a thirty-something stay at home mom with no experience, but I had to start somewhere.

So, I started with the mail. I began opening the mortgage statements, credit card bills and other such postal goodness and came to a startling conclusion, one that I was ill-prepared to wrap my head around or open my wallet to.

Shit wasn't getting paid. At least not for the house. You bet your bottom dollar, and that's about where I was at that point financially speaking, that his apartment was not in the red, but the house was and I was seeing it. He had been sufficiently supporting his bachelor lifestyle for months while shirking his responsibility to his still wife, and son. We were months behind. Thousands and thousands and thousands of dollars in debt. I was barely surviving on the cash tips from my bartending gig and he was living the highlife, footloose, fancy-free and completely fucking me over.

There were times I cashed in change for groceries. Times when I couldn't leave the house because I didn't have money to put gas in the car. And now, to add insult to poverty, the house was on its way into foreclosure – with us living in it.

Not on my cheap watch, motherfucker.

So I did what any self-respecting woman would do. I borrowed money from my brother and hired an attorney. The silver lining here was that I was learning all sorts of new things about mortgages, foreclosures, divorces and court orders that I had never known, nor desired to know prior. My lawyer filed a motion for Pendite Lite support which, in a nutshell means that until we reached an actual settlement, he was going to have to cough up some cash, and quick.

Somehow, the concept of supporting one's family had eluded my ex and he was raging fucking pissed that he was now required to provide funds to help pay for trivial things like food, clothing and shelter.

I'm fairly certain that once I played the money card, in conjunction with the fact that he was, at this juncture, in the midst of an unhinged and unrivaled bender, he was going to go off the fucking deep end, and that is precisely what happened.

Throughout this child support shitshow, he was drinking heavily and had recently been ordered to undergo supervised visitation in order to maintain my son's safety. There were instances of neglect that I don't even want to think about and, in order to protect my child, his visitation became limited and supervised. All the while, this asshole continued adamantly asserting his sobriety and simultaneously refusing to cooperate with court orders. He was being a cunt.

Then, one fine day, after receiving confirmation of yet another incidence of his driving under the influence, I put my foot down and refused him contact with our child, who was only five years old, and incapable of advocating for his own health and welfare. Enter crazy person, stage left.

Before I provide you with a play by play of the sixteen hours that followed, let me offer some simple yet pertinent advice to the general public regarding electronic communication. If you don't have anything nice to say, don't say anything at all, particularly if you are going to communicate it in a manner that is in writing and admissible in a court of law. Don't use your work email address to solicit prostitutes on Craigslist, don't use your smartphone to sext-message underage girls, and don't use your iPad, which is likely synched to your children's photo galleries, to send dick pics. Don't. Don't. Don't. You fucking idiot, don't.

Between 11:06 AM one damp and dreary day in March three years ago, and 2:19 the following afternoon, I was the lucky recipient of a vomit-inducing series of harassing text messages, phone calls and emails. I can still feel the chill that was in the air that day when I recall how it felt to be on the receiving end of such a disgustingly, hate-fueled tirade and I shudder to think that I ever allowed myself to be treated in such a way.

Here are the highlights:
"You miserable, maniacal money-whore. Bloodsucking piece of shit." 1:33 PM
"You are a fucking piece of shit. You are the most selfish, self-serving cunt I have ever met." 7:06 PM
"You useless piece of shit of a human being." 7:08 PM
"Fuck you." 7:16 PM
It was hardly half past dinner time and he was already dropping the c-bomb. Jesus Christ.

Buckle up, it gets worse. I'm sure by this time of day, the rate of alcohol consumption had rapidly increased and, as expected, the quality and quantity of messages were directly affected.
"You fucking piece of shit whore." 7:21 PM
"Fucking psycho." 7:22 PM
"You lazy piece of shit. Fucking piece of shit." 7:56 PM
Let me also qualify the insanity of this conversation by noting that the only time I had participated in this one-sided douchebag diatribe was at 7:10 PM, when I kindly asked that he not contact me anymore. Apparently, he did not get that message.
"Fuck you." 8:30 PM
"You motherfucking piece of shit." 8:41 PM
"Fucking cunt." 8:41 PM

Probably passed out for a little while, then awakened to the realization that he had yet to drive his point home.

"You are such a piece of shit." 11:02 PM

"Yup, still a piece of shit." 11:58 PM

"You're such a piece of shit." 1:52 AM

"Oh by the way, did I mention what a cunt fucking whore you are lately? Piece of shit motherfucker and worst mother to a child there is. You piece of shit." 2:19 PM

OK, let me see if I understand. So, what you're saying is I'm a piece of shit? Got it. Thanks.

Maybe the reason the word cunt pissed me off so much was how sporadically it was used, unlike the indiscriminate, insurmountable application of the "piece of shit" references. I have to give credit where credit is due, because I certainly did feel like a piece of shit that day, but he was the one that was going to feel like a total cunt when I got finished with him.

I want to make something abundantly clear. Nobody deserves to be treated like this, ever. Nobody should fear the sound of their phone ringing. No one should lie awake at night listening for the rustle of gravel shifting under tires in the driveway. A woman should not feel the need to check the locks on windows and doors, over and over and over again with the fear that, the next time there will be someone other than herself in the reflection of the glass. There is no reasonable rationale for such repulsive behavior, for harassing someone and inflicting emotional distress or fear for one's safety.

I was drunk, is not a valid reason. I was angry, is not a valid reason. I was hurt, is not a valid reason. I heard every excuse in the book, but the single, true reason for speaking to someone in this way, for calling them a cunt, is that you, in fact, are a fucking cunt.

After that very long and painful evening, and a very long and painful trial, I secured myself a very lengthy and painfully necessary Final Restraining Order, and by lengthy, I mean for the rest of my life. No contact, no excuses. No bullshit. I remember, when the judge issued her verdict in the case, that she indicated her belief that even with this order for no contact, she believed that he was capable and likely to harass me again. So far, lucky for me, he has not. This order is the shining achievement of my divorce because it is the one state regulated safety net that is actually effective and enforceable, unlike child support and alimony, in case you're wondering.

I sat through my ex touting his newfound sobriety, his asshole mother lying and crying, and a bitchy, conservative defense attorney making me feel almost as piece of shit-ty as he had, but it was worth every cringe-worthy second since I'll never be made to feel that way again.

The moral of the story here is simple. Don't be a fucking cunt, and unless you are a stellar, Aussie comedian like Jim Jeffries or a fierce bitch of a Real Housewife like Erika Girardi, don't use the word either.

An amicable divorce may be something nearly unattainable, like Hamilton tickets or a dignified presidential candidate, but it is possible. I think.

14: On the House

Suggested pairing: Angry Balls

I had the good fortune of stumbling upon this delicious concoction at a local bowling alley, while on a playdate. Definitely a strike of the spirit variety.

1 shot Fireball Whiskey

1 pint Angry Orchard Cider

Fill pint glass with Angry Orchard. Fill shot glass with Fireball Whiskey. Drop shot into beer and enjoy. Try not to get pissed, drunk, or piss drunk.

Cheers.

There are many aspects of this stunningly ridiculous situation with my ex that really piss me off, as you may well imagine, but I make every effort imaginable to not exist permanently in the realm of bitter, hateful bitchdom. While I admittedly experience fleeting moments filled with revenge fantasies and well thought out, then promptly deleted email rants, I have become fairly accomplished at deflecting bullshit and being the bigger person, since I never get to be the bigger asshole.

I expect little and that's what I get with regard to physical, emotional and financial assistance in caring for our little boy. This is what makes me see red. And what, may you ask, have I gotten in the way of help this month? Not one, red cent

Throughout my ride on this crazy train, I have had the privilege of familiarizing myself with the inner workings of the judicial system via countless trips to the county court house. The senior gentlemen security guards smile and greet me upon entering. They scan my belongings, allow me to leave my coffee on their counter and, kindly inquire, "You know where you're going, right?" Sadly, I do. Meeting with a probation officer with regard to child support? 1st floor on your left. Restraining order? You came to the right place! Third floor, second courtroom on your right.

A domestic violence advocate will take your information. Custody issues? No problem! There are a number of courtrooms and judges to choose from. Lien on your bank account because your idiot ex failed to pay an electric bill, and you failed to recall that his name was still on your checking account? Make a right and see the clerk at the window. Oh, there's so much to experience! Slap a name tag on me and call me your fucking tour guide.

Now, I don't like to play favorites, but of all the courtrooms in the house there is one that never fails to wow me. With its endless assortment of colorful clientele, and truths stranger than fiction, Child Support Enforcement Court is the place to be. On any given day, typically Friday morning at nine, one can bear witness to an astounding display of incompetency and idiocy. Each drama, uniquely sad and pathetic, plays out like its own daytime soap opera. There is often crying, sometimes yelling, rarely paying, and it's never ending. Everyone's short on cash but no one is short on excuses.

Here's the rundown of what happens at an enforcement hearing. The hearing officer takes attendance, calling the names of all plaintiffs and defendants. Many of the defendants are not present. When a case is called, the details of the case are read to the hearing officer and both parties are sworn in. The officer then speaks with both parties regarding whatever questions, comments or complaints may be relevant, and this is where it gets interesting.

There is a specific reason that Child Support Enforcement is my most favorite court in the land, and that specific reason is actually a specific person. On one glorious Friday morning last year, I had the misfortune of having to attend a hearing, but the good fortune of encountering a new hearing officer in court. My ex arrived that day in his usual fashion. What he lacked in punctuality he made up for in presentation, sporting a crisp grey suit and matching tie, as well as a fresh haircut. Under normal circumstances, he is able to fool even the brightest individuals into believing his deceptions, and schmooze his way into the hearts of ignorant women abound. Not today.

On this day, he encountered his nemesis – an intelligent, independent woman fluent in bullshit with a proclivity toward doing the right thing. She had a fondness for the forthright and a penchant for prudence. This was not his day.

Upon being read the particulars of the case, she paused, lowered her glasses, looked the defendant dead in the eyes and asked, in an effort to clarify and possibly condescend, "You owe HOW MUCH in arrears, sir?" Finally! Someone shared in my disgust and disillusionment. But it didn't end there.

She continued to interrogate him as to his apparent inability to establish a consistent work history and to provide for his son. She probed as to why he was up to date on his own rent and utility bills but months, maybe years, behind on providing for his son. She questioned as to how he was able to afford health insurance for our son when he only works two days a week, and when he stated that his parents funded it, she replied "And you are how old, sir?"

He was stunned, and so was I, but for markedly different reasons. She had delivered a deadly one-two punch combination and he stood staggering awaiting the final blow. Oh, and you bet your bottom dollar, she delivered. She ordered him to pay a lump sum of money by month's end, of several thousand dollars of the total arrears owed. And down he went.

He said that there was no possible way that he could make such a payment and inquired as to what would happen if he failed to comply. She explained that if he did not make the required deposit, a warrant would be issued for his arrest, to which he replied indignantly, "Then issue the warrant." She said "O.K."

At the conclusion of each hearing, the officer informs the parties that if they are unsatisfied with the order for any reason, they may contest the ruling and go before a judge for a judicial second opinion. In true douchebag form, he had the audacity to do so, and on to the next courtroom we went, only to receive the exact same judgement as we had from the kick-ass and take-names hearing officer.

The final act of this shining shit-show came when we were exiting the court, for the second time, and a kindred child support spirit approached me in the hallway. She said, "I just wanted to tell you that I thought I had it bad, but that was the worst I've ever seen here." Wow. As my mom would say, "If I weren't so proud I'd be ashamed."

Needless to say, we all saw red that day. I did when he arrived looking like a million bucks and having zero. He did when he realized that if he continued to hurt our son by not supporting him, it would eventually hurt him as well by landing him in the slammer. The hearing officer saw red when she saw him and all of his arrogance, incompetence and indolence coupled with his haircut and hangover. But where does that leave us?

Years ago, when my grandfather passed away, our family had a conversation in the car while waiting to enter the cemetery for burial. My dad expressed his wishes to be buried as well and wondered aloud where his final resting place might be. Reflecting on my dad's wishes, in addition to his lifestyle of hoarding the remains of busted coffee makers, damaged televisions and fragmented lamps and alarm clocks, I offered up the only logical burial plot. I informed him that we would put him in a box marked broken daddy and leave him in the garage with all the other stuff that doesn't work." I'm glad we have a solution for the broken daddy when he's gone, but where do we put the broke dad while he's still here?

God forbid we put him in jail so he can sober up.

15: Free Pour

Suggested pairing: Victory Brewing Company Cage Radler

A citrus lager that pairs well with kicking ass.

1 bottle of beer

Actually, make that 1 case of beer

Serve chilled, garnished with an orange slice if you like, after ruffling feathers and rattling cages.

Cheers.

For all that I lack in technological ability, organization skills, brain to mouth filter, whiskey consumption and the capacity to feign liking anything including, but not limited to lamb, chocolate, certain bureaucratic aspects of my job, social situations with any more than three attendees, and people in general, I'd like to think I make up for in vocabulary.

I like words. Like, in a super nerdy kind of way. The enjoyment that certain individuals experience reading gossip magazines, horoscopes, trashy novels and asinine tweets is gained, for me, via a thesaurus. #wordswithnofriends.

You never know when or where the next new-to-you dictionary definition may slap you across the face. Prime example: My current favorite word, albeit an urban dictionary entry, is thickums, about which one of my students graciously educated me. By definition, thickums are girls who are a little bigger, but in a good way. Thickums are also serious producers of "Thicotine" which, according to my unofficial informational source, "keep the boys coming back for more." You're welcome for that little gem.

I also recently learned from a colleague that a quagmire is not only a complex situation and a character on Family Guy, but a soft area of grass that gives way underfoot. Well, giggity, giggity.

There is a certain level of gratification in finding the perfect word. I have perseverated for hours, unable to complete a comprehensive written thought, perusing the inner nooks and crannies of my brain for an exceptionally effective expression to replace some mundane, cliché term in an effort to illustrate my point in a specific and superb fashion. I have written and rewritten, edited and revised, wondered, pondered and obsessed in order to comprehensively communicate my innermost thoughts and feelings to the outermost edges of the blogosphere. Albeit frustrating, there is unfathomable and unexplainable fulfillment in composing an unsung symphony of vernacular, that which results in a lingual masterpiece.

I am fully aware that one man's trash is another man's treasure and, while I may produce something I believe to be the written equivalent to Beethoven's 5th or the non-existent script to Vanderpump Rules, you may think it is complete shit, just as you may assert that my favorite Bravo show is shit, and you are entitled to your opinion, as wrong as it may be.

Remember, beauty is in the eye of the beholder, bitches. And just like I may not be able to appreciate your weird pregnancy photo shoot or your Instagram filtered photo of a meal from last night, we all have our artistic preferences.

In any event, as I stated prior to a sincere and heartfelt shout out to Jax and Stassi, I really love language. I read the word of the day online and try to incorporate new vocabulary into everyday conversation. I'm a dork, whatever. I like layered speech and plays on words. I live for games such as listing various "isms." One time, I managed to momentarily wake from a beer, travel and toddler induced coma just to contribute the term pulmonary embolism, to one particular Atlanta-based, family edition of the ism game. Go me. I thoroughly enjoy absorbing new information, engaging in thoughtful conversation and pushing the boundaries of opinion and so-called knowledge. Every lesson learned is a small victory, so far as I'm concerned.

I like to know things. I want to know things, therefore, I do not buy into the notion that ignorance is bliss. My son's father and his parents, however, wow. They bought stock in that shit. They sell that theory as far as they can despite the fact that no one around here is buying anymore. They are truly the Billy Mays of Bullshit. They have their heads so far up their asses I'm honestly surprised that they do not function in a perpetually circular shape. Contrary to their modus operandi, I think ignorance is stupid, or...well, ignorant as it were.

The stupidity of this situation is significant but self-propelled. The specific district of Crazytown that my ex resides in is built upon a unique foundation of arrogance and ignorance, one that has created such a fortress of solitude that even an adorable eight-year-old cannot penetrate it. Stubborn as I am, I decided recently to attempt, one last time, to initiate an impeccably planned invasion on my son's behalf, in order to coerce my son's father out of Crazytown and back into the Parent-Hood.

Fortunately for me, my mission and my word bank, this battle cry came in conjunction with a handy-dandy addition to my linguistic repertoire. While I maintain a few go-tos when discussing my ex, there is nothing better than learning a term that sums up a situation to perfection. Now, if Roget had a better term for douchebag than douchebag, then I would surely invest but, to be fair, it's fitting and fantastic, and I love it. However, when initiating what has proven to be the most tactically challenging forward movement in our fight thus far, I had the pleasure of being introduced to what I deem to be the utmost fitting of terms for my present mission and potential outcome: A Pyrrhic Victory.

Allow me to explain just how I came to know about the PV.

At the beginning of November, around the time that my child support arrears had reached a maximum, my patience a minimum and my son asserted that his desired interaction with his father is shooting him in the balls with a Nerf gun, I decided to file a motion in Family Court. I'm no dummy, but I'm no attorney either so I sought the advice of a dear friend and damn good lawyer: she was my divorce lawyer to be precise, and when I say damn good, I mean that her unofficial slogan should be "don't fuck with me."
And you shouldn't.

In a series of text messages, I outlined the mission of my motion and she suggested that I be clear with my intent and also give my son a Wet Willy from her. I heeded her advice on both counts and went to work.

But shortly before doing so, she simultaneously expanded my vocabulary and narrowed my focus by informing me of the likelihood of the specific type of victory I may encounter. Essentially, a Pyrrhic victory is one that is won at such a great cost that it is tantamount to defeat. Basically, there's a good chance that I'm going to go to court and win on paper, but I'll be giving up so much shit it won't even matter.

But it will to me, and here's why. What I am asking for in my court motion is only what is already owed, ordered or outright deserved. What I am giving up in my court motion is pretty much anything I can in order to accomplish that.

Long story short, I am requesting that the court uphold orders already in place for overdue child support in an amount that would surely make you shit, counsel fees for the aforementioned awesome attorney and, last but not least, enforcement of an existing order for supervised visitation. Yes, you read that right. I am asking the court to force my son's father to spend time with him. I am such a bitch.

In order to sweeten the deal for the defendant, I have volunteered several suggestions as to how to make this a win-win situation, however pyrrhic it may turn out to be. I have agreed to relinquish my right to the hefty sum of alimony on the account, in addition to taking on medical coverage for our son in order to keep it consistent and up-to-date. Essentially, I am giving up half of what we are owed in order to get half of what we are owed, and I'm beginning to see the basis of the "tantamount to defeat" argument Why am I doing this? The simplest answer to this question is that I have no choice.

At this juncture, the relationship between my son and his father is so fractured, I'm uncertain if there is any hope at all of repairing the damage. But if I don't try, I'll never know and I owe my son more than that. I am willing to put in the effort that his father refuses to in order to give my boy the best chance at a functional relationship with a dysfunctional parent. He may not have the best dad in the world but I'm hoping that's better than not having one at all.

So, I learned how to type a family court motion, pro se. And a certification. And a notice of motion. And a case information statement.

I learned how to cite case law. And support guidelines. And statutes.

I made photocopies. And tabbed exhibits. And mailed envelopes. Regular and certified. And here we are today. 572 copies, 17 exhibits, 2 trips to the post office, 2 visits to the courthouse, 1 check and a self-addressed stamped envelope and countless hours later.

The victory, however pyrrhic, is in doing this on my own. It is confronting the situation head on, hoping for the best, and accepting whatever the outcome. It is in being honest and having hope, and I'd say that's a victory in and of itself. I may lose on every count but at least I'll go down swinging in my son's corner.

It has been said that "victory belongs to the most persevering," and I think that is the notion of the motion. The victor is not the one who yells the loudest or hits the hardest. The victor is neither the one with the strongest words or even the best intentions. He is certainly not the one with the biggest ego or smallest contribution. Victory belongs to those who are faced with unimaginable obstacles and somehow manage to overcome. It belongs to those who fight uphill battles and find success against all odds. It belongs to those who discover strength despite struggle and develop integrity amongst adversity.

Victory belongs to my son because he puts one foot in front of the other and presses on. Because he continues to grow and move forward, even when having to do so uphill, and his success is the sweetest victory imaginable.

16: 190 Proof

Suggested pairing: Everclear

If you require additional proof that you are a raging alcoholic, then you've come to the right place.

Everclear. That is all.

Cheers.

Rollercoasters. The pride of the amusement park and adrenaline junkies. Hair raising twists and turns draw thrill-seekers back, time and time again. F that. I prefer my feet planted firmly on the ground and my stomach where it belongs: decisively affixed within my midsection, not in my throat.

Oddly, I exist primarily on a ride of this sort, despite persistently affirming my fear and loathing of electrifying attractions, and wondering sometimes if I even meet the mental height requirement for riding. The rollercoaster I'm on was designed by a junkie driven by something other than adrenaline, however, and I really, really want to get off. But I can't.

This weekend was the Six Flags of shit. Crazy shit. Crazy shit that I don't want to have to deal with anymore, but somehow, I'm along for the ride. It's as though I'm in line, on crutches, and I get unsolicited VIP access straight to the front. And, we're off!

I had been looking forward to a fun Friday evening out for quite a while. It had been a solid six months since I had experienced a night sans son. A glorious, childless evening to revel in fleeting adult company and to indulge in my brothers' favorite ism — hedonism. And, so I did. Unfortunately, though, negative experiences with another's alcoholism makes hedonism less likely to be achieved, and nearly impossible to be appreciated.

Sadly, upon embarking on this voyage, I came bearing my typical single-mom baggage – stress, anxiety, guilt, pressure, etc. It needed to be perfect because it would likely be so long before it reoccurred. It could have been, had I only let it.

I am seated, front row, sweating bullets, safety harness tightly fastened. As we slowly ascend on the rollercoaster, we enjoy wine, oysters and eclectic atmosphere in a small, historic village. Thanks to a generous Airbnb gift certificate and a nominal Visa gift card, our accommodations and first round of snacks and bevvies are on the house. We quickly and apprehensively approach the first drop – and this one is full of excitement and exhilaration.

The reason for celebration, the first arm-raising, ear-piercing shriek of this ride was pure joy and a sense of freedom. Friday, at 11am, I officially filed for Bankruptcy. Woooohoooooo! Chapter 7, baby! Oh wait, is that weird? Is this not a reason to rejoice? Is this not something that normal people become animated about? Too bad for them, then, because I feel like a rock star. I'll explain why a little later. Back to the initial decent of the rollercoaster ride.

Anyone who exists as a single parent fully comprehends the fact that no good deed goes unpunished, and no good night out goes untarnished. The single parent likely being the offending party, and I surely was. Dammit. I can't even have a good time while specifically out to have a good time. What is wrong with me?

We drove to a bed and breakfast in a small town in Pennsylvania, just far enough away to feel disconnected, and just close enough to be available if necessary. It was beautiful, and quaint, and exceptionally peaceful. And haunted, by the way, but luckily I was not privy to that information until the following morning. We arrived around six, checked in, and promptly Uber'd it into town to have dinner and drinks. Guided by a recommendation from a friend, we cozied up to a friendly bar with great service, delectable appetizers and wine by the glass that would make a bottle jealous.

After a heavy pour and a light meal, we traversed to our next destination to meet friends. I indulged in a Bailey's and coffee, partially to fulfill my stamina needs but mostly to meet my whipped cream quota. Well on our way, we were on our way to our next stop. We arrived at the much anticipated local Speakeasy to find it too full to accommodate four at the bar, and onward and downward we went, to a little place known as "The Funhouse." I wish I could say it were fun, but I can't. And I only have myself to blame for that.

I often forget, or fail to acknowledge, that on my quest for all things adult, I disregard the fact that there is sometimes another individual embarking on the ride with me. I subconsciously place so much pressure on myself and the evening to have a good time that I make it nearly impossible to do so. I become agitated and argumentative, and admittedly, a raging nightmare to be around. The self-indulgent argument ensues, and I find myself in a similar position to being at home with a child – frustrated, at my wits-end, only this time resulting in the parent requiring a time out. I behaved like a petulant child, one who wishes for the world to revolve around them – their feelings, their rules, their demands. How absurd and how selfish.

Everything bothered me. The talking, the drinking, the general fun-having. This is supposed to be enjoyable, so why am I making it so miserable? Yet, I can't stop. I was such a raging bitch, even I wouldn't want to hang out with me, and I find bitchiness endearing. I couldn't get out of my own way long enough to absorb a fantastic rock band singing Taylor Swift, nor could I step out of my mind for a moment to bust out some sweet dance moves and kick it with some kick-ass people. And then comes the Jägermeister, like a burly, idiot friend who comes along to avenge you when you've done something astonishingly moronic. Thanks, buddy.

Somehow, in spite of myself, I managed to come back around by the end of the night and enjoy the final hour. I danced, and laughed, and lived for a few brief moments in time. Unfortunately, my rally in the bottom of the ninth does not make up for my poor sportsmanship throughout the rest of the game. I owe my teammates more than that, and I failed them.

As if my behavior weren't proof enough of the baggage and bullshit, the insecurities and imperfections that I carry around from my experiences, I really sealed the deal the morning after with my hangover comprised of guilt and self-loathing. It seems that, on the rare occasion that I truly let loose for a few hours, I spend twice as much time beating the shit out of myself for doing so. I have been so affected by someone else's excessive drinking that, on the rare occasion that I drink to excess, I liken myself to him. I am harder on me than I have ever been on him, maybe because I expect more from me. Not to belittle the migraine quality headache and flu-like sweats and nausea, but my mental state was far more fucked up than my physical symptoms. I hated myself for having fun, and for not being able to actually have any. I hated myself for hating on someone else's good time.

So much proof of how far I have to go in recovering from this.

I hope that the people that I love forgive me for my shortcomings; that they see in me the capacity to overcome them. I hope that they find evidence in my everyday existence to sustain their involvement with me until I am able to fulfill my potential as a human being. But I guess, as they say, the proof is in the pudding. I know the pudding will be delicious, I just hope that when I am capable of truly enjoying it, I haven't driven away the person I want to enjoy it with.

Have you ever had bread pudding? It's chunky and has raisins in it. I hate raisins. The next loop of the rollercoaster made me want to vomit bread pudding. Chunks abound. Raisins shooting out of your nose. Fucking nasty. But in the pudding, lies the proof, and here it comes – out your nose.

On the way home the next morning, I decided it would be a good idea to swing by my old marital residence for yet another epic trip down memory lane. Aside from the fact that it was directly on our way back, it also conveniently coincided with my bankruptcy filing, adding to the psychological urgency to visit there one last time.

Once Monday rolls around and my poor me papers are filed, I will have surrendered this property to the bank, never being able to set foot inside again. In all honesty, I want nothing to do with the house at this point. While beautiful, it has sustained flood after flood after flood, and its turn-of-the-century interior is riddled with black mold and dark memories. The random-width pumpkin pine floors creak with each step and my heart breaks with each movement, as I ponder the could have's and should have's. It was my home, my son's home, and now it stands vacant.

The house endures as a monument to my marriage – empty and abandoned. It is dark and dank and musty, and longs for the attention of a loving inhabitant, someone to see its beauty and potential. But, for me, it is a haunted relic, one I am thankful to be rid of.

If you could have seen this home in its glory days you would have fallen in love at first sight like I did. The grounds were rolling and rich, and the interior exquisite. Exposed beam ceilings and walk-in fire places adorned a centuries old estate, complete with a Jersey Winder staircase and a second story balcony extending from the master bedroom.

I entered the house, in spite of the boarded up entrances and lockboxes on the doors, and in spite of myself and my own better judgement. I entered on the second story. I won't say how, just call me MacGyver. What I discovered was just more proof of what I already knew to be true, of how totally fucked up my ex had become, and how far away I wanted to be from here.

He had evidently visited the residence recently as well, but for markedly dissimilar reasons. An empty wine bottle was left haphazardly in the guest bed alongside a portable DVD player. Clothes hanging in the closet waiting for some ghost of his past life to dress up and come alive. Torn pages from a 70s era Playboy Magazine were littered across the upstairs living room floor, in a disturbing crescent arrangement, as if we'd arrived just after he'd left. It was bizarre.

Bottles. Porn. Cobwebs. Mold. I felt like I was in Hester Moffet's storage facility in The Silence of the Lambs. It was creepy and eerily lived in, as though I had just narrowly missed the previous occupant. As if I needed more proof of his drinking, more proof of how disturbed he had truly become. Why did I come here? Closure before the foreclosure. Too soon? Never!

I left the house, for the last time, and I am never going back.
To add insult to injury, and crazy to creepy, when I got back in my car, I had a text message from his most recent ex-girlfriend. Oh, good lord, perfect timing. We just hit the first loop on the ride, the one that makes you throw up a little in your mouth, and wish you hadn't jumped on board in the first place. Ironically, on the same evening that my friends and I had the joy of revisiting a few of the residual issues that cling to my back like a drunk monkey, my ex was parading his problems about as well.

He had gotten into a fight. At work. He'd been fired. Fired from a part time server position. The only position he'd been capable of holding down over the past few years. This ride just doesn't end.
I guess I won't be holding my breath for child support this month, or in the hopes that he's getting the help he so adamantly claims he is. The evidence says otherwise. More proof. Unbearable quantities of proof. Moonshine level proof.

Proof of his perpetual downward spiral. Proof of his drinking and lying. Proof of what I already knew to be true. Proof that I really don't need any more proof.

The evidence is always there. On every liquor bottle, and on the face of every active alcoholic. Sometimes the proof is nominal – a 10 proof can of Budweiser. Sometimes it's 95% alcohol by volume and you're dealing with the Everclear of never-clear. The truth is buried beneath so much bullshit, that you struggle to reconcile what is fact from what is fiction.

This life will bankrupt you, financially and emotionally. When the addiction takes a fierce hold, priorities skew from child support and mortgage payments to bitterness and bingeing. It proves exceptionally difficult to bounce back from these bankruptcies but, each day we move forward assists us in rebuilding our credit. While I sometimes encounter reminders of my bad credit history regarding marriages and mortgages, debts and divorces, I use them as motivation to do better, to be better.

There is nothing wrong with filing for bankruptcy, just as there is nothing wrong with cutting loose once in a while. There is freedom in finding the courage to change the things we can, even when it seems impossible. It is only then that we may experience the serenity that follows. It is through these experiences, positive and negative, successes and failures, truths and lies, that we gain the wisdom to know the difference. If I've found proof of anything worthwhile, it is that bankruptcy is not the end.

It is the beginning.
It is the beginning of a wild ride of my own design. And I'll be first in line for that son of a bitch, proof positive.

17: Holiday Spirits

Suggested pairing: The Nog

My mother was given this recipe by a coworker over forty years ago. It has become a deliciously drunken family tradition.

6 eggs separated

1 ½ cups brandy

6 cups milk

cream

Nutmeg

¾ cup sugar

½ cup rum

2 cups heavy

Beat yolks until light and fluffy. Add sugar and continue beating until blended. Slowly add brandy and rum, then milk and cream. Beat egg whites, in a separate bowl, until stiff and fold in. Add nutmeg to taste.

Cheers, and happy holidays!

Just before Christmas, a friend of mine initiated a group text featuring a trio of martini glasses, informing all included that we would be visited by three spirits. A short while later, another festive friend blasted out a cutesy, chalkboard-type holiday decoration, aptly adorned with the phrase "It's beginning to look a lot like fuck this."

Turns out, both sentiments were true.

The number of spirits may have been a slight underestimate.
The greatest joy of the Christmas season is experiencing it through the eyes of a child. My son marvels at the twinkling of lights and brightens at the prospect of snow. He anxiously awaits the arrival of family members, near and far, in addition to the possibility of a package on the porch each day after school. He looks forward to the family Nerf wars, as we look forward to the family Egg Nog.

He carefully decorates the tree, making quite sure that the vast majority of the ornaments are placed in one giant concentrated area, eye level for him, and chew level for the dogs. List after list is written and revised, with the Santa-directed requests becoming more intense and less feasible. The magic of Christmas becomes hypnotic, creating an insane yet innocent belief that Saint Nick can create toys that don't exist because, after all, he has a workshop full of elves who, much like the desired toys, are a work of fiction. I have to give it to him: his imagination is infinite, unlike my finances and my patience.

Still, despite the endless lists of gifts to wrap, rooms to clean, food to cook, stockings to stuff and cards to mail, the magic of Christmas remains because the children forever keep it alive. Until they discover Santa isn't real and their parents have been lying to them for their entire lives. Can't wait for that mind-blowing, gut-wrenching, soul-crushing realization. It seems the only silver lining of this inevitable holiday heartbreak is that we won't have to deal with the Elf on the Shelf any longer.

This fucking elf is the bane of my existence, I swear to Santa. If I have to wake up just once more at three o'clock in the morning to move that fucker because I forgot to do it before bed, I just might lose my mind. In fact, I am beginning to believe that the asshole that invented this god-forsaken thing didn't do so to teach children the beauty of big brother government surveillance, but did so rather to destroy the minimal amount of sanity parents cling to during the holiday season. But, I digress.

Back to the holiday spirit, and spirits.

While having the pleasure of witnessing my son's wide-eyed wonder regarding everything Christmas, I also had the good fortune of being reminded, myself of the true meaning of holiday spirit. Though this reminder may have come in liquid form, and the Christmas spirit who visited may have been slightly under the influence of egg nog, it was still a lesson worthy of aide memoire.
Despite all of my meticulous planning and attention to detail, I was surprisingly unprepared for my holiday schooling and subsequent visits from the ghosts of Christmas Past, Present and Future.

While I was fully prepared to Nog it up, as we say in our family, I was not expecting any additional uninvited spirits. Fortunately, however, their visit came simultaneously as all three ghosts showed up in the form of a harrowing holiday phone call between my son and his father.

Late in the evening, sometime around the twelfth of December, days before my son was to celebrate an early Christmas with his father's side of the family, he decided to call and check on the status of the list he had mailed the week prior. It came as no surprise to me that, somehow, the envelope had failed to arrive after six long days, yet only having to travel three short miles. His father claimed that he had checked his mail and the envelope we had so carefully addressed, had not made it one town over from our residence to his. He insisted that he had never received it and requested that we email him the list again so that he could order them now, even though it would be impossible for them to arrive by early Christmas.

I wanted to blame the United States Postal Service, but even they don't suck as much as my son's father, and that's saying a lot.
Needless to say, my son was devastated. Immediately following the phone call, he asked to use my phone so that he could check on the exact name of the action figure he wanted from Amazon.com. Evidently, the one and only action figure he wanted from his father was a limited release, and no longer available anywhere online. To say that he was disappointed would be a redundant understatement. No fake phone call from the North Pole, no unexpected Xbox would ever make up for the daddy disillusionment that had just slapped my boy upside the head.

He sobbed.
And screamed.
He proclaimed his hatred for his dad.

And how he only ever asked him for one thing, and he couldn't even do that.

He furiously asserted his awareness that his dad has done nothing but let him down his whole life.
And how he wanted to kick him in the balls.
I sobbed.
And agreed.
I held him tightly until he fell asleep with a broken heart and a tear-stained face.
And then I went on EBay.
Fortunately, there were two of this particular toy remaining on a seller's site in Oregon, and we were able to order one just in time for Christmas.
But what about early Christmas?

After careful consideration and a glass of Egg Nog with the Christmas Spirits, I was reminded of what it is like to see this day through the eyes of my son.

The Ghost of Christmas Past reminded me of how difficult the holidays have been for a young boy, whose ultimate Christmas wish for a functional father will likely never come true. This spirit retold the stories of the last few Decembers from my son's point of view. He talked of sadness and fear and disappointment. He spoke of a boy who wants a daddy.

The Ghost of the Present chimed in and shined a light on the Christmas miracle I had sitting right in front of me - the opportunity to give my child the most beautiful gift a mother could. This spirit reaffirmed my belief that in every bad situation lies a silver lining, sometimes you just have to be humble enough to find it.

The Ghost of Christmas Future showed me so many magical holidays to come, me and my boy, and how much happier we would both be year after year. This spirit encouraged me to do what was in my heart for my son, and reassured me that we would both reap the benefits, today and all days.

I took my last sip of Egg Nog and toasted to the Christmas spirits and I began to write.

I wrote to my son's father. I, again, told him of the one thing he had asked for this year. I also told him that it was no longer available to order because he had waited so long. And then, with as much spirit as I could muster, I offered him the chance to give our son the toy he wanted so badly. That is, if it arrived on time for early Christmas. And it did.

That afternoon, I hugged my son and sent him off with the other, less awesome side of his family. I sent him with good tidings and cheer, and the action figure he so desperately desired, neatly wrapped with a gift tag that said "Love, Dad." I sent him off with a smile on my face and joy in my heart, knowing that this would be the best early Christmas ever.

My son's happiness was the greatest gift I received this year. He believes in Santa Claus and the Elf on the Shelf and, however little, he still believes in his father. Someday when he is older, the magic of Christmas will be a distant memory, and the same might be said for his belief in his father. But not this year. Not this day.

My boy still marvels at the twinkling of lights and brightens at the prospect of snow. He still hears the hooves of reindeer on the roof and sees Santa's sleigh in the night sky. He knows not of the behind the scenes exertion necessary to make these dreams a reality. He does not need to know, not yet.

Someday, he will understand. He will understand that mom is Santa, the Elf on the Shelf, on occasion dad, and has been kicking Christmas ass and taking names for years. At some point, he may no longer believe in Santa or his father, but I'll be damned if he won't still believe in the spirit of Christmas.

18: Neat

Suggested pairing: Foolproof Brewery, Queen of the Yahd IPA

A delightfully refreshing, raspberry infused brew that will put a crown on your head and a smile on your face.

Bottle

Opener

Open bottle, consume and get royally shitfaced.

Cheers.

There is a fifth dimension beyond that which is known to patrons. It is a dimension as vast as space and as timeless as infinity. It is the middle ground between customers and cocktails, between assholes and alcohol. And it lies between the pit of man's pollution and the summit of his sobriety. This is the dimension of intoxication. It is an area which we call The Bartending Zone.

Imagine if you will a full bar. Patrons abound, happily sipping wine and martinis, politely awaiting your attention. The conversation is light and the atmosphere relaxed. Everyone smiles. Nobody waits. The bartender is the ringmaster of a fully functional adult circus. Then, suddenly, something goes awry. There is a malfunction in the well-oiled inebriation engine.

Service tickets spew from the machine at an unrivaled pace. A keg kicks while a glass is simultaneously broken in the ice bin.

The rate at which glasses become clean and dirty skews and a flood of "excuse mes" and "can we get another round" nearly drowns you. At this precise moment in time, two new clients arrive, well-mannered and well-dressed, eerily too much so for this particular establishment. In a futile effort to appease, you approach them with service and a smile, and inquire as to their intended beverage. Their response is deafening. "I'm not sure what I want. Surprise me." And so the bartender's nightmare begins.

I admittedly, on more than one occasion, have made the mistake of actually honoring this request. I should have learned after the initial failure but I am stubborn and sometimes forgetful. I make a slamming Bloody Mary. I don't typically toot my own horn, but toot, toot motherfucker, it is delicious. I am adept in this art, not as a result of extensive training on the subject, rather my own personal enjoyment in consumption. I like vodka. I like tomato juice, lemon and horseradish. I especially enjoy the accoutrements that frequently garnish this cocktail: olives, celery and, on a rare and glorious occasion, bacon. It is a meal and it is magnificent. It is the bevvie breakfast of champions. But not everyone shares in my enthusiasm.

Despite my passion for the drink and precision in its construction, many patrons do not wish to indulge in this fine concoction. It is imperative to remember that in bartending, like most aspects of life, our tastes are not shared by everyone. We each have unique tastes, spanning from appreciation to disgust. I will never again surprise someone by imposing my preferences upon their palette. If this request is presented, I will graciously produce a glass of water for them to enjoy until they change into their big girl pants and choose a beverage their own. To quote a timeless Bush-ism, "fool me once, shame on you. Fool me – you can't get fooled again."

I make the best Bloody I've ever had, and I've had many. My recipe is not a secret, not one passed surreptitiously down through generations. It is just mine, tailored to my taste alone, and perfected through mouthwatering trial and error. But as delish as it is, some people just don't dig them. Our penchants for particular liquors are based upon various elements including perception and experience. I don't know why I like vodka, I just do. I am fully aware, however, of the reason I do not like whiskey and tequila. If you have every puked up a certain type of alcohol, then you are undoubtedly privy to the perseverance, and possible masochism necessary to attempt that specific spirit again. I don't do brown liquor. Not ever. Well, a rogue tequila has managed to sneak through following a flock of vinos, but I've stepped up security. No brown liquor I say! As we mature and become increasingly self-aware, we should all apply our perception and experience to acting all grown up and confidently asserting our right and ability to choose our own shot. Let us vow to make educated decisions so that we don't get fooled again.

Take a moment to apply this infinite wisdom to other important decisions. A young, attractive client enters the bar, proudly arm in arm with her stallion of a boyfriend. He is tall, dark and handsome, and his bulging biceps are on display for all to envy and enjoy. She bats her eyes coyly acknowledging his sexy beastness, and I quietly throw up a little in my mouth. While she adores him and all he has to offer, just as I worship my wine, I don't get it. Not my cup of Twisted Tea, so to speak. Utilizing past experience is an invaluable tool in ensuring that we don't reorder the same unappealing drink, and furthermore, avoid re-engaging with an undesired partner.

Alpha dogs and arm candy just aren't for me, so I choose not to include them in my sampling of significant others. Varied taste is a positive human adaptation because otherwise we would all invariably be chasing the same dude, and the same keg of beer would always be kicked. I am capable of appreciating aspects of another entity without necessarily finding them attractive. Attraction and appreciation are not one in the same so, while one may recognize my affinity for all things bloody, our affection remains divided.

I will not be bamboozled by booze. I will not allow another's indecision to deceive me into poor decision. Never again will I trick myself into believing that a relationship I know to be unhealthy deserves another round. I will NOT ingest brown liquor. Just as I will not be duped when it comes to my own, or someone else's social or alcohol consumption, I will not be misled regarding my ex's denial of his own. "Fool me once, shame on you. Fool me twice, shame on me." This mantra has been relentlessly battered into me by his belligerence and his bottle.

Over the course of the past few years, my son's father has had limited and supervised contact with our son. Praise the higher powers of the higher court, my interaction with him is nearly non-existent. Our "relationship" consists of the exchange of an alcohol screening swab prior to supervised visitation. Long ago, I conceded to the fact that he exists in an unending spiral of substance abuse. Despite deep denial and indignant assertions otherwise, he is an active and raging alcoholic.

Contrary to several stints and rehab and a mid-blowing accumulation of DUI's, he denies the issue with consistency and conviction. His refusal to admit he has a problem is only rivaled by his refusal to submit to a breathalyzer. Taking these fucked up facts into consideration, in order to ensure safety, it has become essential to scientifically determine the level of intoxication at the time of the visit. Common sense dictates it should be zero. Common sense also dictates that this is a relatively simple feat when said visitations are scheduled in the early morning hours. He failed. Silly me for thinking he wouldn't.

In my fog of forgiveness and hope beyond hope, my desperate desire to satisfy my son's yearning for a father, I reluctantly brought him along the following week for a refill of resentment and regret. His dad failed the test again. At 10:00 and with flying colors. He seems to abide by the go big, or go home mentality because he lit up that test like 4th of July fireworks, 3 times the legal limit. Did I mention it was 10:00 am?

Admittedly, that wasn't the last time. I know, I'm foolish. It was right around the fool me 7 times, and I'm a fucking asshole mark that I finally got the hint. Think what you will. My intentions were good, but the road to hell is paved with good intentions. Heeding my own advice and acknowledging a disturbingly abundant amount of evidence, I will not be fooled again. I will not get fooled into getting drunk on brown liquor and I will certainly not, not ever again, get fooled by a drunk. If this circumstance presents itself sometime in the future, I will be no fool. I will bestow upon him the same counsel I do my indecisive bar patrons. My recommendation is, and will always be, to just drink a glass of fucking water because, trust and believe, the Bloody I am capable of unleashing on you is not going to go down smooth.

19: Bar Flair

Suggested pairing: Bartender's Choice

Because I'm the boss.

Order anything colorful, fruity, unreasonably annoying to make, and derived from ridiculous bottle juggling and excessive, unnecessary shaking, stacking and flipping.

Cheers.

I have been asked many, many times while bartending if I knew any good jokes, funny stories or bar tricks. This is an annoying question because, first and foremost, with the exception of Tom Cruise in Cocktail, a bartender is not a trained circus animal, and second, the answer was always no.

I can remember the phone number of a 7th grade teacher whom a friend and I prank called one time, but I can't remember a fucking joke. Not one. And even if by some miracle of science or aligning of the stars, I happen to recall a portion of a funny ha-ha, I totally screw up the punchline.

Fortunately for my patrons, as well as my own sanity, I somehow managed to pick up one kick-ass bar trick along the way. I wish I could remember who taught it to me but, par for the course, my memory fails me. I do recollect the handful of times I have performed it, and each was magnificent.

The most recent sighting of this elusive and exceptional bar trick was two years ago around the holidays. While out for drinks with family and friends, the topic came up and one of my brother's acquaintances was happy to oblige. He presented a variety of gags, none of which I remember because none of which were memorable, yet he'd captivated his interested, albeit intoxicated audience.

My brothers and I had cashed out and were on our way to the door when I decided that this was an opportune time to bring my favorite trick out of retirement. I approached the young man like a wolf in sheep's clothing, asking permission to participate in the festivities. I informed him that I only had one trick up my sleeve and he graciously and condescendingly accepted my request to perform it, with him as my magician's assistant. Let the games begin.

I began by politely requesting two pint glasses of water from the waitress, to which she kindly indulged me. Upon the arrival of the waters, I instructed this gentleman to place his hands flatly and firmly on the table, betting him that he couldn't balance the two glasses on the backs of his hands. He was certain he could, and so was I.

It is a delicate process and an admirable feat to successfully balance two overflowing 16 ounce beverages on someone's body, especially after both parties have had their fair share of cocktails, but it was a shining success. He stood there anxiously awaiting the next direction and said, "So, now what?" To which I replied, "Have a good night"

As we turned tail and made for the door, all that could be heard in the distance was the rousing laughter of onlookers followed quickly by the shattering of glass and pride.

The beauty of this trick is in its simplicity. It proves astonishingly simple to deceive someone when they are none the wiser of the punchline of the joke. Conversely, it is extremely challenging to dupe someone who is at all times acutely aware of the objective of such deception. Simply put, you can't bullshit a bullshitter, and likewise – you can't out bar-trick a bartender.

Outside of the consequential shattered glass, it did feel good to get one over on someone who never saw it coming. That being said, it feels really shitty when someone, successfully or unsuccessfully, attempts to get one over on you.

Throughout the course of my ex's alcoholism, I have become increasingly equipped in predicting and preventing the various types of fraud he has attempted to execute. On occasion, however, he catches me off guard with his black magic and sends me into a tail spin. But once I learn the trick, it's game over. Fool me once, remember?

In the event that my son's father wakes up before noon and has the wherewithal to lucidly communicate with his son and, furthermore, actually show up to a visit, I have the alcohol swab tests ready and waiting. He can try all sorts of trickery to deny drinking: lying, producing forged AA attendance logs, etc. but he can't beat a swab test.

Oh, but he'll try.

In one example of his pathetic attempt at parlor tricks, he tried his hand at beating the house. We were meeting him at the local diner down the street from his apartment so that they could have, what usually ends up being, a 40-minute breakfast with redundant dialogue regarding swimming, school and the weather.

His swab performance up until this day had been spotty, intermittently passing and failing, while simultaneously destroying my son's mornings. That day, I mentally prepped myself and my son for the possibility that he would fail, again, and the visit would need to be terminated. My son, in all of his devotion, believed in his father. I, in all of my disgust, believed I might kill his father.

We arrived and parked a few doors down from the café and waited. He showed up several minutes later and opened the car door to let my son out. Before they proceeded to their superficial father-son date, I handed the test to him, he swabbed his cheek and handed it back before quickly walking away.

The test was positive. Again, between two and three times the legal limit positive. At least he's consistent.

I yelled for him to come back and he ignored me. He brought my son into the restaurant and I hauled ass to catch up. I confronted him at the table with the failing test grade and he, never deviating from his go-to reaction, implicitly stated it was impossible.

This time, however, he tried out a new trick he had up his sleeve, but it was a juvenile effort at outwitting both me and the test.

"I used Listerine just before I left. That has alcohol in it and must be why the test came out positive". Nice try asshole.

Funny thing about these tests is that, really the only thing that can create a false positive is mouthwash. Like a handful of my students who are naïve and sometimes rather lazy and complacent, my ex initiated a google search and failed to move beyond the first three results. If you're going to try to pull a rabbit out of a hat, at least have the decency and dedication to conduct research that extends farther than the paid web pages.

You can't out bar trick a bartender, my friend.

I pretended to be an enthusiastic audience participant in his show and offered to bring back another test to prove his theory, and his sobriety, knowing full well who the bullshitter was in this act. I conceded to the possibility that his morning dental hygiene routine had, somehow, disrupted our dysfunctional family outing.

Out the door I went, and immediately into the pharmacy down the block. I retrieved a bottle of Listerine and swigged a mouthful, enough to make my eyes tear from something other than disappointment and deep disgust. I spit and sped home to wait an additional ten minutes before testing myself to see if it would still detect the alcohol in the rinse. Shocker, it did not. Totally negative. Back to the diner I went, full of rage and minty fresh.

Door to door to door, he'd had a minimum of 50 minutes to expunge the gargle from his body. He'd also had the opportunity to ingest a full breakfast to soak up whatever non-liquor based alcohol he claimed to be the culprit.

He failed again. He still blamed the breath freshener.

I proceeded to beat him at his own game, outlining the efforts I'd exerted to disprove his idiotic hypothesis. I'd found the poorly disguised false bottom in his magician's hat. But like a good magician, he refused to reveal his secret.

We left, prematurely terminating the visitation, and devastating my son for the remainder of the day, and several that followed.
My ex has a real flair for bullshit. He really isn't any good at it but, man, does he practice. He regularly attempts disappearing acts, both with himself and money, and continues to try and perfect this cheap parlor trick, endeavoring to cover up his obvious intoxication.

His magic show is in town seven days a week, but I am no longer in attendance. I've seen all of his tricks and I know his secrets. Unfortunately, the only trick he has been able to pull off successfully is making his relationship with his son disappear.

Ta-dah.

20: Shitfaced

Suggested pairing: Pinot Noir

Why, you ask? Because I drank a ton of it when this shit went down.

Recommendation: Irony Pinot Noir. For obvious reasons.

Cheers.

Ever have someone shit on your driveway? Nope, me neither. As the ex-wife of an alcoholic, I have had many aspects of my life shit on. He has taken a shit on my trust, my self-esteem, finances, and my son's emotional well-being. All things being equal, he has never taken a shit on my driveway. Proverbial poop and literal driveway defecation exist in two wildly different universes. Evidently, he was saving up this dynamic deuce for a partner of a later date. Lucky for me, sucky for her. Now, I've heard of a lot of crazy shit in my life, pun intended, but this is new. I must give credit where credit is due, because there isn't much that really shocks me anymore, but this one? Holy shit.

I actually know someone who would purposely and maliciously crap on someone's property. I was actually married to this person. Not exactly dating site material or something to write home to mom about, sad but true. Now, I don't know what that says about me as a person, and frankly I'm not sure what it says about you if you're still reading this, but here we are.

What's disturbing about someone else's alcoholism is that no matter how far away you go, it inescapably finds its way back to you. Even when you are wholly removed from the day to day life, if you can even call it that, of a raging alcoholic, you are always anxiously awaiting the other shoe to drop. Alcoholism is the Carrie Bradshaw of diseases. There is always another shoe, and that fucker is always going to drop. There was a 5-inch Jimmy Choo banging down my door this time, and let me just tell you, I wasn't exactly happy to see it.

Per evening protocol, I was enjoying a cigarette, a glass of wine, and a brief adults-only conversation. These are fleetingly delicious moments to savor in the life of a single parent. No sooner had I settled into a glass of Pinot Noir and a relaxing summation of the day's events, had my phone buzzed with a new Facebook message from a name I recognized, but a motive for contact I did not. And so it began – my shitty spiral back into his addiction, this time with his girlfriend as a copilot.

"Can you please tell him it's in his best interest to leave my neighborhood? He was not invited over and is just hanging around and because of the ladder incident from before my neighbors are not too understanding of him."

Hmmm. This is either a conveniently ironic mistake-a-message intended for another recipient, somehow landing in my hands following a 50-yard field goal attempt by the humor Gods, or this is the second in a pair of plummeting Jimmy Choos. The latter is the most obvious answer. The latter it was, but, the ladder? I wondered about this ladder incident among a million other futile grasps at rational thought.

I came to understand the latter and the ladder, and the shit in the driveway. And all of the other events that I have worked tirelessly not to have to cope with. I may be hardened to the plight of an alcoholic, but I empathize deeply with that of the individuals that inevitably become their collateral damage. Without a second thought, I re-engaged in his crazy. I figured she's either a moron or a masochist. Of course she is, just as I was, and still am in many ways. As well as a compassionate, trusting, selfless woman, who sees the best in an addict despite their constant and consistent reassurance of the many reasons not to. She is a mother. I could not, in good or any conscience, turn my back to her, even if that meant relapsing into his bullshit. And so I did.

I engaged in conversation. I rehashed emotions. I compared stories. I called his parents. I considered calling the police. I prayed. I cried. I went to bed. I learned of the incident last summer, reminiscent to tonight's stalking events, though that particular evening included a ladder climb, attempted second story break in, and an eventual call to police. It also encompassed, as I recognize from my own admitted enabling behaviors, as well as tonight's happenings, a moment of weakness, forgiveness and subsequent regret. I woke up the morning after with the same hangover from this crap I'd had years ago, many times. Too many times.

While I played this crazy game with his little lady, he worked his own alcoholic agenda. He banged on the door, yelled through the windows and harassed her until he eventually gave up. He left her house and left her alone, but not without incident, and not without a fight. And not before taking a crap on her driveway, and a crap on my sane, sober-from-him day.

Well, shit.

He may as well have lit it on fire and left it on my front porch.

21: Top Shelf

Suggested pairing: Top Shelf Margarita

Because you deserve it, you badass motherfucker.

2 ounces Anejo Tequila

1 ounce Grand Marnier

1 ounce fresh squeezed lime juice

1 ounce orange juice

Sour Mix

Coarse Kosher Salt

Lime wedge

Fill cocktail shaker with ice. Add tequila, orange liqueur, lime juice, orange juice and sour mix. Shake until chilled and combined. Wet rim of margarita glass and edge with salt. Pour mixture into glass, garnish with lime and enjoy.

Cheers.

Sometimes a situation calls for a bevvie of extraordinary prestige. A wedding necessitates a champagne toast. A new job elicits a celebratory happy hour round of drinks. The birth of a child, well breast milk, but wine on reserve for the new mom – she'll surely need it. All of life's great moments feature a complimentary cocktail. Baseball game? Beer. Ladies night? Cosmopolitans. Bachelor party? Ugh, Jägermeister. Every reason for getting shitfaced is accompanied by a standby spirit. So, what's the occasion for the Top Shelf Margarita? Irony. Irony is the fucking occasion.

A Norman Rockwell painting we are not. As I sit, seething, typing this at my parents' kitchen table, my son is happily cozied up with his father on the couch in the living room, watching the Transformers movie he rented On-Demand, that I will assuredly be footing the bill for. They relish in a bowl of popcorn together as Bumblebee and Optimus Prime kick ass, and I fume yards away, dying to do the same.

Sadly, this is to be the highlight of my son's week. Pay no mind to the summer off with mom packed with rainy day movie excursions, spontaneous trips to the city, swimming with friends, the Firemen's Fair. Those are all fine and great, but they are peanuts to a dad visit. I bring the peanuts, and dad provides the elephant in the room. What a circus.

From an outsider's perspective, this afternoon appears to be an average, All-American family day. The house is clean and orderly. The family unit together under one roof – mom in the kitchen, dad in the family room with son enjoying a laid back summer day. But mom and dad are divorced and do not speak. Son is on his absolute best behavior with dad because he knows not when he will see him again. The house belongs to the grandparents and is used as a neutral ground for supervised visitation.

These father-son visits are supposed to be conducted in a therapeutic setting, facilitated by a clinical psychotherapist, at a weekly frequency and a rate of $175.00 per hour. My request for reinstatement of these office visits was rebuffed due to a recent employment crisis for the king of financial fuck-ups.

Since he was fired from his fancy-pants restaurant gig for what he claims was an altercation with a co-worker, when in actuality, he was fired for showing up to a dinner shift drunk, he can no longer afford to fund the therapy. Not that he was doing that to begin with, because his parents were. In reality, until he secures yet another fleeting server position, his mom and dad are footing the bill for his child support each week.

This guy knows how to work the system. He ignores the compounding arrears and the growing cost of feeding, clothing and caring for our boy, and deposits the minimum payment required monthly to keep his ass out of jail. And that's exactly what his parents are doing now. Nobody seems to give a shit when my son grows out of his sneakers every other month, or needs antibiotics not covered by insurance or requires individual counseling once a week for a significant out of pocket fee. There is no urgency when I have to pay for rent, and electricity, and food, and school supplies, and haircuts and dentist appointments, and school lunches, and summer camp, and before care, and everything else we need to survive. Nope, nobody mails a check then, but when a bench warrant is on the horizon, trust and believe that money will make its way into my account. But not without a struggle.

When news broke of my ex's newfound unemployment status I was surprised. I wasn't surprised that he was fired, I was surprised that he managed to keep this job as long as he did, to be frank. What did catch me off guard, however, was the subsequent request for my help in the child support department. Evidently, if I needed the money to support my child, I was going to have to figure out a way to get it.

The email I received from my ex was short and to the point, almost matter of fact, which further added to my fury.

"As I mentioned before my parents will be helping with the payments until I get a new job. I do not have a bank account so I cannot cash a check they send me and they do not want to mail that much cash.

Would it be possible for them to make the check out to you, we meet at a bank and you cash it then I will walk over to the court and make the payment?"

Hold on. Let me get this straight. He wants me to drive to him, deposit a personal check in my bank account, give him the cash, let him walk away with it, and trust that it will end up in my child support account? I'm a lot of things, but I'm not fucking stupid.

There are a litany of things that piss me off about this particularly bottom shelf experience. First of all, I am not a bank. I have not accepted a position as his personal concierge in an effort to secure a nominal child support contribution. I have enough to keep me busy between my full time job and my full legal custody without having to launder money for Mr. I Don't Have a Bank Account.

In the amount of time it took him to conceive this crackpot idea, type the email, and wait for my response, he could have successfully secured another job. It's not like we're talking about resumes and interviews here. It's an application and an apron and you can likely start that day. Give me a break. I've worked enough years in restaurants to know there's always a job available around the corner, but they don't come knocking on your door to hire you. In addition to the obvious, the inability to cash a check really struck a nerve for me.

He doesn't have a job. He doesn't have a bank account. He's a grown man. What the fuck? The reason that this is exceptionally aggravating stems from a fiscally based email from a previous date and time. Earlier this year, as I changed jobs and residences for the betterment of my son, I received a similar message from my ex regarding said child support, only this time, he wasn't figuring out how to get it to me, he was threatening to have it taken away.

He took this Cuervo golden opportunity to chastise me about child support and all things monetary. Evidently, in his expert opinion, because I made more money this year, he should have to make less. My hard work and dedication had finally begun to pay off, and now he wanted a pay off as well. He actually said that because I had a real job, he shouldn't be required to provide the allotted child support amount anymore. By that logic, I should quit my job for a gig at McDonald's and cry poverty so that my child support goes up. Classy.

A real job. Now I am being punished for having a real job. If he would get himself a real job, we wouldn't be in this sad state of affairs. Maybe if he wasn't always wasted away again in Margaritaville, he'd be able to maintain a real job and sustain a real relationship with his son.

And here we are today. In the family portrait Norman Rockwell would have painted had he used a Groupon for one of those places that people go to drink shitty wine, and create shitty copies of paintings. It's a drunken disaster in every sense of the word.
I sit here typing, grateful for the material yet sorrowful for my son and hateful towards his father. He sits on the other side of a wall and at the end of an alternate universe. I put on a brave face and he puts on a show.

The only major stipulation for these visits, notwithstanding actually showing up, is that he pass an alcohol swab test. I don't ask much anymore, standards have dropped from top shelf to bottom, and he really just needs to be sober 12 hours prior. Sad, I know.
In a strikingly similar fashion to the Listerine incident, he failed three between 10:30 and 1:30.
Three.

Yet he insists he is not drinking. He swears. He hurls insults and AA attendance sheets at me. The tests are wrong, he says. He skirts the issue and tries for the sympathy vote, claiming he was so sick last night with an ear infection, he almost ended up in the hospital. How could he possibly be drinking if he was so sick, he asks? How could he buy alcohol with no money, he questions? He accuses me of wrongdoing. I must have touched or tampered with the test in an effort to falsely implicate him of this heinous act. He sleeps.

Yes, he went to sleep. Rather than spending an ounce of quality time with our son, he nodded off during the remainder of the Transformers movie. He must be extremely fatigued from all of the work avoidance and story-telling.

And the fun didn't stop there. Let's have another round, shall we? Shortly after he left I received an email with another ridiculous request. Apparently the validity of all three swab tests had come into further question, and he wanted me to conduct an experiment, like I did with the Listerine. So shocked he was by the obvious scientific failure of the tests, he wanted me to swab myself the next time I had popcorn to see if that results in a false positive. Popcorn, he stated, was the only thing he'd consumed in the last 24 hours so there must be some top secret shit going on at Pop Secret. Oh my god, I feel crazy.

Even more disturbing is that a part of me actually buys into this insanity. For a moment. It's a very short trip from Margaritaville to Crazytown in my world these days.

I wonder how the hell we got here. I wonder how he got this bad. I wonder if he truly believes his own lies. I hope it gets better. But until then, I hold out hope for him and his recovery. And I hope that the next time he spends his money on the makings of a top shelf Margarita rather than his own child, as he sips it, the wisdom of Jimmy Buffet comes to mind.

"Some people claim that there's a woman to blame,
And I know, it's our own damn fault."

22: 86

Suggested pairing: The Hemingway Special

Because if you're Ernest fucking Hemingway you get a drink named after you. Maybe someday people will be doing AA Ex shots for me. Maybe not.

2 ounces white rum

1 ounce Blue Curacao

2 ounces pineapple juice

1 ounce grapefruit juice

Splash of lime juice

Splash of Grenadine

Pour all ingredients into shaker over ice. Shake until chilled and combined. Serve in a chilled glass over crushed ice. Be like Hemingway: "drink to make people more interesting."

Cheers.

I am putting the world on notice that I have officially had enough. I have had enough of my ex and his unrivaled ability to do absolutely nothing. I have had enough of seeing my son grow up without a functional father. I have had enough of always following the rules and doing what is right and having my efforts met with the exact opposite. I have had enough of refused visitation, ignored emails and withheld child support. I have had enough of hearing sob stories, seeing my son cry and smelling bullshit.

Enough is enough.
But when is enough really enough?

I know for sure when enough is enough with regard to a few things is. Three glasses of wine is enough. Conversely, three cups of coffee is also enough. Four Advil is enough. Unless, of course, three glasses of wine didn't seem like enough the night before. One Polar Bear Plunge is enough. Four dogs is enough. A job that fulfills me, a house to call home and a family to love is more than enough.
I am also well aware that there are certain circumstances that arise when enough is never truly enough.

The first and most obvious is cheese. As far as I am concerned, there is never enough cheese. Ever. The remainder of the never enough category has become increasingly more obvious and equally impossible to ignore as we get older and wiser and acutely aware that the time we have on this Earth will never, ever be quite enough.

Ernest Hemingway once said, "Try to learn to breathe deeply, really to taste food when you eat, and when you sleep, really to sleep.

Try as much as possible to be wholly alive with all of your might and when you laugh, laugh like hell. And when you get angry, get good and angry. Try to be alive. You will be dead soon enough."

I am earnestly practicing Ernest's proposal of breathing deeply but, lately, my deep breathing has been more like huffing and puffing and wanting to blow a certain someone's fucking house down. I breathed in, filed a 150-page court motion, and breathed out. I breathed in, anxiously awaited his response and didn't get one, and breathed out. I breathed in, anxiously awaited our court date, only to learn that the judge would rule without oral argument, and breathed out. I breathed in, and now am holding my breath for the order to arrive in the mail, and I'll keep you posted as to when I have the opportunity to breathe out.

Ok, so the deep breathing exercise, like all forms of exercise, seems to be something I have yet to master.

With regard to the second and third aspects of Hemingway's revelation, however, I am a fucking rock star. Tasting food I have locked down. Whether it be a bag of Cape Cod chips and a bowl of onion dip, a cheese plate, a sushi boat, a medium sized bag of movie theater popcorn or a gallon of Turkey Hill Cookies and Cream ice cream, trust and believe, I got this. I live for food. I love it, I cook it, I dream about it and I will eat pretty much anything and taste the shit out of it. Hemingway would be so proud of me. I sure am.

The one and only thing that trumps food is sleep, and sleep trumps everything. I like to think that I am experiencing motherhood sleep karma at this stage in my life. For the vast majority of the first four years of my son's life, he didn't fucking sleep. Like ever. When he did, it was for approximately two to three hours and/or while I was holding him. Have you ever tried sweeping floors with a broom in one hand and a slumbering infant in the other? It looks idiotic and proves unproductive, but it does strengthen bicep muscles and single-parenting skills. My one-armed baby bandit days are over though, and I am absolutely making up for lost sleep.

My sleep schedule begins no later than nine pm each evening and lasts until six o'clock in the morning. That's right bitches, I sleep for nine hours a night, sometimes more. Nine glorious hours of uninterrupted, restful bliss, and I have earned every single second of them. I don't care if "Making a Murderer" is on television, or if my best friends are having drinks at my favorite restaurant or even if there is a personal chef and a professional masseuse knocking at my front door; if it's happening after nine o'clock, it's not happening with me.

Trying to be wholly alive, however, is easier said than done. We are all so busy and burdened with bullshit, sometimes being wholly alive is enough to kill you.

Existing is not at all the same as living. We exist day to day, waking up, going to work, running errands and repeating until the days we are alive become a blended string of successive repetitions with little to no meaning whatsoever. That is, until the universe throws a wrench in the machine we call life, and forces us to take inventory and take notice. These worldly wrenches typically come in the form of death, and rattle our sense of security and viewpoint on values. Nothing reminds you of what's important quite like losing someone who is just that.

A year ago this past October, we took in a twelve-year-old rescue dog whose owner had died. He was a gorgeous Chow-Rottweiler mix from Pittsburgh who was in danger of being put down, and I couldn't stand to see that happen. Fast forward a year and here we were with an elderly dog, and a looming likelihood that he would have to be put down, this time by us.

He had begun to have difficulty breathing and walking, and I was left with no choice but to bring him to see the veterinarian. The prognosis was poor and he was in pain, and I left that day with a heavy heart and an empty passenger seat. I also left that day with an overwhelming sense of guilt and a gut-wrenching emptiness. I left asking myself over and over if I had done enough. And the truth of the matter is that I hadn't.

Yes, I took him in when he needed a home. I cared for him when he was ill. I gave him kisses and hugs and treats galore. I spent time with him when I could, and loved him like I love our other four dogs. I loved him enough to let him go.

But it wasn't enough, because when it comes to love, it is never enough.

Too often, we take for granted how fleeting our stay is in this world. We disregard the rapidly ever-shortening calendar on the wall and maintain our position in a futile race to the finish, where we all realize the same fate. We forget to slow down and take breaks and appreciate the simple and the beautiful. We love each other, but naively expect that we will be granted an infinite timeframe to express that love, and when the door closes, we are sad and angry and empty. We are slapped across the face with the harsh reality that, not only was our time with our loved ones not even close to enough, no matter the amount, but also that we hadn't done nearly enough to appreciate them while they were here.

Being wholly alive, as Hemingway proposes, requires that we be present and positive, grateful and available. We should be our best at all costs, for ourselves and for the ones we love so much.

Sometimes it proves damn near impossible to be our best, especially in the face of adversity or in the wake of loss. These are the times when it is essential to remember the "laugh like hell" component of Ernest's eloquence. Laughter has become the best medicine for me. Maybe this is because I'm Irish or maybe it's because I can't afford therapy but, whatever the reason, humor is my go-to outlet for coping with crap. We should laugh at struggle, and stress and shitty ex-husbands. We should laugh at family conflict, and funerals and fucked up situations. We need to be able to laugh at our failures, our losses and, most of all, ourselves.

The anger part I have down, but I am becoming increasingly frustrated with myself for being angry lately. I am making half-hearted attempts at forgiveness and good ole Christian love thy neighbor shit, but I have yet to be successful in this department of self-destruction. I am angry. "Good and angry," as a matter of fact, and it doesn't seem to be getting me anywhere at all except, of course, more angry. I feel spiteful and vindictive, and a need to prove a point to my ex about where he has gone wrong and what he needs to do to fix it, and even though I dress these desires up as a warrior in my son's army, in reality, it's just a little girl crying over spilt milk. And again, this makes me angry. But I think I've been angry enough for a lifetime, and it's time to move on.

And so this brings us back again to being alive, which is what I intend to be for quite a while, but despite having the best of intentions, I might not be. Whether we are here living for a minute, a year, a decade or a century, we need to be alive and aware of the fact that our time will never be enough. We need to do enough and love enough and live enough to make the most of the moments we have.

We should hug our children and hold onto our parents. We should build lasting relationships with friends and Legos in our basements. We should read books and write them, and leave legacies of love and progress. We should say what we feel, say what is true, and say the f-word for fuck's sake. We should be honest and kind. We should be brave and bold, and a force to be reckoned with. We should be here now, be ourselves and be thankful for every second we are given to do so.

We need to be the best parents, the best children, the best siblings, the best friends, and the best all-around versions of ourselves as possible because, eventually, we won't be anything but a memory. Do everything you can as thoroughly, thoughtfully and thankfully enough as possible because, truth be told, enough is never going to be enough.

So, my advice, based upon Hemingway's advice, is to live. Eat the cheesecake. Pick up the phone. Kiss goodnight. Dance on tabletops. Forgive the assholes. Stay up late. Love everyone. And forget sleep trumping everything. We can all sleep when we're dead, and according to the Hemingway Special, we'll all be dead soon enough.

23: Pick Your Poison

Suggested pairing: Snakebite

You won't NEED to pee on yourself as a result, but there's a good chance you'll probably end up doing that anyway.

1 part Jack Daniels

1 part Tequila

Pour ingredients over ice and shake until chilled. Strain into a shot glass.

Cheers.

There comes a point in all things alcohol when we reach a proverbial fork in the road. Are we ready for another round, or is it time to cash out? Somewhere in the neighborhood of wine number three, a silent alarm goes off reminding us that the next one may not be such a smart move.

It is at this moment that we are forced to choose whether to belly up or bow out. In brazen contradiction to the DEFCON 5 alerts in our minds, set off by the internal mechanisms furiously hitting the abort switch, we occasionally succumb to our stupidity and indulge in "just one more." Only one more multiplies like rabbits and, after a bevy of bevvies, gives birth to belligerence, promiscuity and the dreaded drunk dial. Dammit. The choice to move from round three to round four becomes exponentially more difficult the more we consume, as does the choice to get drunk or get sober. But we all need to pick our poison – pick being the operative word. After all, it is a choice, isn't it?

The topic of choice came up while sharing a story about my ex and his sobriety, or lack thereof, this past week and it got me thinking. After adamantly defending my disgust with his behavior, I carefully began considering the other side of the debate. To what extent is there a choice to drink or not to drink when it comes to alcoholism? Hop on my train of thought and come along for a ride.

Step one of the 12 Steps of Alcoholics Anonymous program states that "we admitted we were powerless against alcohol." Seems legit, but I have to be honest, I'm slightly perplexed. Utilizing this statement as the foundation for our current dialogue, I find that there are two possible applications for this declaration. Alcoholics exist in two mutually exclusive groups: those who are actively engaging in substance abuse, and those who are actively disengaging from substance abuse. An alcoholic who seeks treatment has accepted that they have no control over their substance abuse. An alcoholic who refuses to assent to the need for treatment also has no control over their substance abuse. If we have no power, how do we have a choice?

I do not believe that alcoholics make the choice to be alcoholics, just as I do not make the choice to have anxiety. You would have to be some kind of stupid to choose a life affected by either of these conditions. I do believe, however, that alcoholics have the ability to choose sobriety over substance abuse. Consider, if you will, that if we concede to the idea that this entire population of people has no power over their illness, then we equate the sober individuals to their drinking counterparts. Doesn't this negate the strenuous efforts employed by those who have "chosen" abstinence? If the alcohol truly has the power in this instance, then is it the alcohol making the decision to not drink?

Control and choice appear to be the underlying facets begging to be addressed. If it comes down to command over one's actions, then how do we qualify and quantify control? Is it even possible? Alcohol abuse is a compulsive, addictive behavior, typically influenced by an intermingled set of dynamics including genetic predisposition, environmental factors and psychological conditions. Smoking fits the same characterization. I smoke. I know I shouldn't but I do. I am aware of the health risks associated with this addiction, and yet I continue to do so. My parents smoked, so possibly I am genetically predisposed to this behavior, or likely I was impacted by external environmental factors that taught me to deem this addiction acceptable. I smoke because I am stressed, I can't imagine why. All things considered, I can quit if I want to. Yes, that is the standard smoker's response to people when they reaffirm the shitty side effects of this behavior. No, I probably couldn't quit tomorrow, but that's really because I am not ready to and, quite frankly, don't want to right now. 16-hour marathon as a single parent? Smoke 'em if you got 'em. No money in the bank? Light 'em up, Johnny. You are actually on the phone with your ex's ex talking about him taking a crap in her driveway?! Give me a fucking cigarette – in fact, give me the whole pack.

I concede to the fact that quitting smoking would prove extremely difficult at this stage in my crazy game, but I will not accept the notion that I am under the thumb of a Nicotine dictator. A challenge is not an impossibility. Let me drop some philosophical shit on yo' ass.

The concept of free will has been a point of contention among philosophers for thousands of years. Are our actions a function of our volition or are our outcomes predetermined by a fixed set of universal fates? Throughout the course of this deliberation, the theory of free will has been closely associated with moral responsibility. Our actions look to be guided by a fundamental awareness of right and wrong, good and evil. Human beings tend to be equipped with an inherent moral compass, that which assists in our navigation of the world around us. If we aware that an action will cause harm or detriment, and we contend to chart that course, is our moral compass malfunctioning? Are we making a choice to ignore morality or to act in spite of it? In this particular case, is it the individual or the alcohol that has the control, which makes the choice, which retains the will?

Another interesting idea to explore is that of disorder versus disease. These two terms are of similar origin, express analogous meanings, and are often applied interchangeably in clinical settings. So what is the difference? After exhaustive research, I discovered that there is little, if any, dissimilarity at all. I googled, I Bing'd, I DSM V'd that shit and here is what I uncovered.

A disease is a condition that prevents the body or mind from functioning normally, typically manifested by distinguishing signs or symptoms. A disorder is a physical or mental condition that is not normal or healthy. Clinical physicians tend to reserve the latter to reference an issue that is psychological or psychiatric in nature, while the former is often employed in characterizing a physical malady. Essentially, we are the forefront of the old "a square is always a rectangle, but a rectangle isn't always a square" model. The singular, defining differentiation that became apparent is that a disease is a condition that is concrete and clinically verifiable through pathology. Case in point: if you cut someone open, you can see lung disease, heart disease, and liver disease.

An autopsy will not, in contrast, reveal alcoholism, nicotine addiction, anxiety or depression. While one may view their physical symptoms and side effects, the disorder itself will not be visible. Is there a tendency to sympathize more so with alcoholics than patients suffering with other mental illness just because we use the word disease? Is it only worse because we call it something worse? Listen, I know this is some heavy shit. But this is some heavy shit! And, for my own piece of mind, I needed to know that I wasn't being ignorant or indignant, wasn't being wholly insensitive to something I hadn't sufficiently studied. I get that being an alcoholic is not a life that anyone in their right mind would choose. I agree that it is a devastating and debilitating disorder, one that is exceptionally difficult to overcome. I would never belittle a person who is fighting this demon. I do not dispute the difficulty in making the decision to succumb and overcome, to persevere in the face of extreme adversity. I do, however, contend that, though the choice does not exist to have this "disease," the choice is available to fight it.

After drink number three, or four or after you've lost count, the opportunity presents to make the choice and pick our poison. We can live for one more round or one day at a time. We can exhibit control or compulsion. Disease or disorder. That being said, why don't we just call a spade a spade? In the debate surrounding substance abuse and sobriety, are we strictly arguing semantics?

24: Muddled

Suggested pairing: Mojito

When you just aren't sure which drink to order, choose the one that requires the bartender to pick fresh fucking mint from the garden. Oh, and be certain to ask for one in the winter time when it makes absolutely no sense whatsoever.

2 ounces white rum   *Fresh mint leaves*

2 tablespoons fresh lime juice   *1 tablespoon sugar*

Club soda   *Lime wedge*

Zero regard for your bartender's sanity

In a hurricane glass, muddle mint, lime juice and sugar. Add ice, rum and club soda and shake until chilled. Garnish with mint leaves and lime wedge. Go fuck yourself.

Cheers.

Every so often, as I march a path of vengeance and vindication, I am abruptly halted in my tracks by some unforeseen event or words of wisdom that force me to question my thought process, moral compass and modus operandi.

Well, fuck me, if it didn't happen again quite recently, and just in time for the holidays. A Christmas Miracle, one might say, especially for a special someone rightfully on the receiving end of my revenge fantasy rage, and Santa's naughty list coal supply. This particular, let's call it a teachable moment, for lack of a better word and for the sake of my inner educator, came right in the midst of a tour de force bitter, hateful bitch moment that I was riding like a biker chick.

A shout out to one of my favorite coffee mugs: "I'm not always a bitch. Just kidding, go fuck yourself." Full disclosure. I don't think I'm a bitch and certainly not the bitter, hateful variety, but I occasionally accede to the incensed, internal volcano erupting within, and I will not apologize for that. Bearing witness to the persistent inner turmoil of a child really puts a bee in my bonnet, so to speak. Eventually and inevitably, that bitch of a bee is going to sting someone.

Sometimes I want to see this circus in my mind play out until the end. I want the Carrie bloodbath, the Hannibal face gnawing, the Saw – choose between your arm and your life kind of internal conflict. I've been all too often finding myself in a make that fucker pay state of mind, entertaining many a sublime daydream of hand to hand combat, and I certainly don't appreciate being snapped out of it by some wise, thoughtful poet.
And then I was.

While on Facebook, oscillating between maniacal political posts, rescue dogs in need of homes and various annoyances including, but not limited to cringe-worthy ignorance pertaining to the current state of affairs in the Middle East and nauseating engagement photos (Really? These seem highly unnecessary and self-indulgent), my scrolling came to a screeching halt on a quotation that hit just a tad too close to home.

"Justice is the grammar of things. Mercy is the poetry of things."

Frederick Buechner

I wish I were diluted enough to believe that this particular assertion hit a nerve within my inner English teacher but, alas, I have come to know myself too well to bury my head in that particular pit of quicksand. It seems of late that I have become accustomed to bookending my daily language arts lessons and writing workshops with commutes to and from work, wherein my focus and attention strays from traffic signals, pop music and cigarettes to perusing pedestrians for my ex, envisioning him crossing the road and fantasizing about running him over with my car.

I am wholly aware of the kind of person this makes me and, while I may be embittered and embattled with certain moral dilemmas, I am by no means stupid and would never act on such an ignorant impulse. But there is pleasure in the plotting, truth be told.

Anyone who knows me well has undoubtedly heard me assert my desire to either stab him in the eye or run him over with my car, both by accident of course, those two methodologies being my go-to forms of imaginary assault and battery, just as "shit" and sonofabitch are my first lines of combative communication.

Amidst all of this verbal motherfucking and physical shadowboxing, on a quiet evening several weeks ago, after teaching lessons in grammar at work, I was taught, however unwillingly, a lesson in poetry. I was forced to reexamine my perspective and to question my motives. I ended up, through thoughtful introspection and unexpected conversation, reexamining my circumstances and reaffirming my beliefs. To a certain degree, I had been schooled.

I don't particularly enjoy admitting that something so simple could baffle me and leave my entire belief system staggering, and the fact that the blow was delivered by such a diminutive opponent only added insult to injury. In any case, 'twas time for some serious self-examination and reflection.

Maybe I am a bitch.

I may be functioning on a primitive, instinctual level, unable to grasp the figurative meaning of prose, but I want justice. Justice for my son.

I find myself frequently prefacing my moral assertions with "If I were in his position," or "if it were me," but those lines of thinking are frustrating and futile, and accomplish little more than a review of rules followed and rules broken. But I like rules. Rules are necessary, effective and, like literature's societal counterpart, help shit get done and shit make sense. Grammar may be basic and boring but, without it poetry cannot exist. Everything ever written is merely a different combination of twenty-six letters and, without the grammatical foundation to build upon, literature would be a nonsensical mess, much like Donald Trump's presidential campaign and Justin Bieber song lyrics.

Similar to grammar in its structure and stipulation, is physics. For every action, there is an equal and opposite reaction. If you drink to excess, you will likely be hungover. If you get a DUI, you will likely have your license suspended. If you run your ex-husband over with a car, well, you catch my drift. The reactions to those actions are essentially justice and, while you may be begging for mercy while you're vomiting martinis, who says you deserve it?

As they say in preschool, you get what you get and you don't get upset.

This brings us to the poetry, and the variable in the equation that really had me scratching my head. Does he deserve mercy? From me? On one hand, we have the deadbeat, douchebag dad that merits the tire tracks across his back yet, on the other, we have the afflicted, addicted alcoholic. Maybe justice isn't the solution and mercy is the true means to the end.

There are fleeting moments when I do truly sympathize with him and his plight. His life is likely full of demons and destruction and void of any feeling of attachment or sense of accomplishment. He has no bank account, no credit card, no money to speak of, and a dead-end job as a waiter that seems to only propel these circumstances into an abyss of mediocrity and self-pity. He has as many DUI's as I have dogs, an indefinitely suspended license according to the DMV, and insurance premiums that would make the health care industry jealous. He has a revolving door of significant others, no close friends and zero custody of his child. Have mercy!

But, should I?
My mother and I employ the logic of the kicking the puppy predicament when pondering questions of this nature. Puppies are cute and sweet and gentile. Puppies give love and affection and companionship. Puppies sometimes chew shoes and remote controls and shit in the house as well, but does it help to kick the puppy? Does the puppy learn anything from that type of redirection, as it were, or do they just feel remorseful and ashamed and hurt? I believe puppies are worthy of our mercy, even when they've consumed nearly every quality pair of sneakers I have ever purchased.

After much careful consideration and with a clear conscience, I vow to be merciful, to be empathetic, and to be kind from this day forward. I promise to be understanding that sometimes certain negative behaviors will be exhibited, mistakes will be made and tears will be shed by a certain someone in my life. I give my word that I will be tolerant, compassionate, forgiving and patient because, after all, it isn't right to kick a puppy.

And that's just what my ex-husband does to my son, over and over and over.

My son deserves the mercy. He is the frightened, untrusting and dejected doggy, whose spirit has been so badly beaten by his father, his soul is left cowering in the corner, awaiting the next stroke of disappointment by his father, the puppy kicker.

What kind of justice is that?

This lesson in grammar and poetry, justice and mercy, has taught me something poetic, something prolific, something priceless. I will walk my path through life with a renewed confidence in myself and my beliefs. I will drive my path to work with a constant reminder of the grammar and poetry of things, and instead of running him over, I will remember to have mercy. I will have mercy on myself and on my son.

And my car.

25: The Glass is Half Full

Suggested pairing for this reading: Half and Half

This delicious beverage is the alcoholic half-brother of the Black and Tan, which is created using Guinness Stout and Bass Ale.

8 fluid ounces pale ale (Harp Lager)

8 fluid ounces stout (Guinness Stout)

Fill half of a pint glass with Harp Lager. Fill the remainder of the glass by slowly pouring the Guinness over the back side of a spoon.

Cheers.

After what seemed like a never ending week comprised of shortened morning class periods with wild children and lengthened afternoon meetings with their respective parents, I ventured out in the early hours of my Friday morning, for what I feared could be the most draining and disheartening parent-teacher conference of the week.

As I dropped my son off with his grandfather in the wee hours, the chill in the air caught me blindside with its forewarning of the dreaded winter to come, and the foreboding implication that this was to be a more difficult morning than usual.

The commute was short and silent, lacking sufficient time for a cigarette or adequate brain functioning for a morning news program. I arrived at the school just prior to my scheduled time, put the car in park, took a deep breath and ventured in, apprehensive as to what stood waiting on the other side of the classroom door.

The conference began promptly at 7:45am. The woman was kind and soft-spoken, light-hearted and light-eyed. A wolf in sheep's clothing, maybe. We exchanged courtesies and sat in chairs too small, amid a mountain of report cards, data sheets and work samples. At this particular conference, I was not the teacher. I was the parent, and yet I felt more like the child awaiting their chastisement by the school principal. And so it began, with my glass most certainly appearing half empty.

This saintly woman, who somehow has the patience and perseverance to effectively instruct and inspire, compliment and care for, redirect and reinforce, support and shape sixteen angelic and devilish eight-year-old creatures, initiated our conversation by thanking ME for taking the time to meet with her, and expressing her gratitude for having my son in her class.

Well, my glass just got a little fuller.

She inquired as to my concerns, if any, regarding his progress at school and his progress report which, at that juncture, shame on me and my state of perpetual motion, I had not yet taken the time to view. All things being equal and in the spirit of full disclosure, I don't typically give a shit about his performance on benchmark assessments, participation in invalid, ineffective standardized tests or his movement from a U to an S in application of units of measure. I know, I know. Bad teacher, worse parent.

What I do care about is my son's happiness. Is he making strides in his social development and interaction? Does he have friends in class? I pray to God he swings from the monkey bars, giggles with his groupmates and doesn't eat lunch alone.

I am hoping beyond hope that he isn't breaking his pencils anymore when his work becomes frustrating. I am desperately wishing that he is not shutting down at his desk when thoughts of his father's abandonment enter into his mind. I am praying, with every ounce of my being, that he is no longer biting his own arms in rage.

In that moment, that split second following a million silent pleases and prayers and just prior to a torrent of tears, a tiny miracle presented itself in a little classroom, in a too-small chair, where baby-steps are taken and milestones are reached every minute of every day.

"He's doing just great" she tells me in a tone that was sincere and almost matter of fact, as if neither of us should be surprised. And yet I was. Surprised at how much can change in year, how far he had come, and how full my glass was quickly becoming.

His teacher went on to expound on his vast and ever-growing vocabulary. She spoke of his love of graphic novels and goofy dances. She told of his above grade level skills in math and science and social studies, his love of art and affinity for all things creative. My son, despite what seems like a paternal crusade to prove otherwise, is a typical, happy third grader. And a star student, by the way.

She thanked me for providing my son with so many positive experiences to draw upon in conversation and in writing, qualifying her statement by adding that too many children have two parents in the home and little more to discuss than cartoons and video games. She told me that I was doing all the right things and, like a child given a pat on the back, I felt warm inside and nodded, both in acknowledgement and appreciation.

I left that parent teacher conference, the most unexpectedly fulfilling one of the week, with my glass filled to nearly three quarters. I left with tears in my eyes and a sense of peace that I had not felt in what seems like an eternity. I left feeling like a good parent. I left before my son arrived to have one more in a growing series of good days.

When I arrived home last night, haggard but happy, I did finally sit down with a glass of wine and read my son's report card. To my surprise, when I thought I could not be any more fulfilled, and my glass could fill no more, my heart nearly exploded. I scanned each of the subjects and their corresponding measures of progress, searching for a "not meeting grade level expectations," and there were none to be found. Not one. Not one one. Twos and threes, and meeting grade level expectations across the board even, and most importantly, in the social emotional areas.

He follows directions.
He listens attentively.
He works independently.
He demonstrates self-control.
He exhibits a POSITIVE ATTITUDE toward learning.

It was enough to fill all the empty glasses and all the empty hearts and all the empty promises. My glass was full of blood and sweat and tears. And joy. My glass was full of joy. And so was I.

At one point during the conference, I had asked if my son's father had ever scheduled to meet with the teacher and her answer was no. While I was not surprised, I was disappointed. It saddened me to be reminded of how little he participates, how little he cares, how little he does at all to be a parent. Truth be told, however, he doesn't deserve to take any pride in a conversation about our son's success because he is arguably anything more than a failure. He has reached such a sad stage of narcissism and neglect, that the only thing his glass is filled with is booze and bullshit. It may be full enough for him, but he will forever be empty.

As we sit here this morning, with what could have been a massive morning hangover, I write and he reads, newfound loves for both of us; the two of us nestled cozily together in front of the fireplace. I look at him with overwhelming pride and joy at the little person he has dared to become in light of his fine attributes and in spite of his father. I look at him with an admitted sense of accomplishment that I have, in fact, done something right. I look at him with wonder, with gratitude, with love.

I look at my glass, and it is overflowing.

26: POS System

Suggested pairing: Flaming Asshole

Because our piece of shit justice system doesn't do anybody justice.

½ ounce Crème De Menthe

½ ounce Crème De Bananes

½ ounce Rum

½ ounce Grenadine

Layer ingredients in shot glass in the following order: Grenadine, Crème De Menthe, Crème De Bananes, and White Rum. Ignite before serving, and try not to set yourself on fire.

Cheers, asshole.

Typically, when a bartender buys you a drink, it's their way of saying "thanks for not being a dick" or "you're a really generous tipper" or "I kind of feel like I have to because you're so much of a regular that you essentially pay my electric bill every month." In any event, if you ever find yourself in a situation where you are offered a drink on the house, be sure to thank your server because, contrary to popular opinion, the bar you frequent, like the world, does not owe you a damn thing. Please don't ever ask for a freebie and, for the love of God, don't expect one just because you've gotten one in the past. That is not the way the system works.

Or is it?

Logic dictates that your obligation as a patron, and as a semi-functional member of society, is to pay for your own shit. Despite what you may have been raised to believe in this age of irresponsibility, indolence and entitlement, the world owes you zero because you're no more fucking special or worthy or needy than anyone else.

The vast majority of us are going to live wonderfully average lives with ordinary families, regular jobs and run-of-the-mill homes and vehicles. Almost none of us will ever own a Lamborghini or trend on Twitter or win the lottery. We will exist, day to day, in the beauty and simplicity of normalcy, and we will pay for all of our average shit with our average paychecks and, on average, will be contented doing just that.

We have learned through life experience that want and need are issues independent of each other, and that both require hard work and discipline to fulfill. We know that having children is life's greatest blessing as well as its most outrageously overpriced accomplishment. We are aware that on any given day our cars may break down, our relationships can unravel and our jobs will fucking suck. These are the reasons why God created wine and also the reasons why we must bust our collective asses in order to overcome such adversities.

But for all of us out there kicking ass and taking names at life, there are a handful of outliers, intent on using their powers for evil instead of good, leeching off of society and manipulating the system to work in their favor.

These are the deadbeats. These are the regulars who expect a free drink. These are the Flaming Assholes.

Allow me to direct my attention to you, you spoiled, lazy, useless excuses for adults. I would like inform you that you cannot spend your life waiting for that big break, the easy way out or for the world to right itself around you. I want you to know that if you refuse to take responsibility for your actions, there will be consequences for those actions or inactions. I am here to tell you that if you fail to meet your obligations as parents, a swift wave of enforcement will sweep down on your ass because our court system is a force to be reckoned with. I am telling you that you must work hard, honor your obligations and take care of your shit, or else.

And now, I must confess, none of that is actually true.
Not one fucking word of it.

You can pretty much do whatever the fuck you want, with whatever disregard for the rest of us, and nothing bad is going to happen. Nada. Do your thang, deadbeats!

Just in case you lack even the nominal initiative necessary to confirm your inalienable right to be a loser, I'm going to do you a favor and outline things for you, real simple-like, so even morons like yourself can figure out how to beat the system. And by the way, this advice is on the house.

You know that pesky child support obligation that's always getting in the way of taking your girlfriend out to dinner and buying yourself a cheap bottle of vodka? It turns out that words like obligation and mandatory are merely recommendations, or glorified pleases from your friendly neighborhood probation department.

Rest easy, asshole, you're not actually obligated to pay this money, you're merely obligated to consider it. "But I have a bench warrant status on my child support account" you say. "If I miss a payment, I will surely be arrested!" Bullshit, I tell you. Here's the skinny – you may notice that warning pertaining to your child support payments and you may, for a moment, shudder with distress and dismay. Have no fear, you flaming asshole! I'm about to drop some information on your ass that is sure to surprise and delight.

Here's how the bench warrant process works, in a nutshell. Say, hypothetically, that you have a proven history of purposefully and maliciously manipulating the child support system by circumventing the stipulations placed on your account. And say, for example, that the mother of your child has gone to great lengths to encourage you to do the right thing for your child, by way of court motions and probation hearings. And say, according to the court's orders, that you now find yourself in a situation where missing one payment could land you in lock up. Relax, it likely never will.

I hope you're taking notes because this is some seriously life-changing shit.

First of all, once a payment is missed, the probation department will kindly send you a letter asking, yet again, for you to fulfill your obligation. Next, when you don't respond, which you won't because you're a dick, they will wait a full ten days before calling you and, again, kindly asking you to fulfill your obligation. Then, when you still don't, because you're a lazy fuck and a poor excuse for a father, they will initiate the warrant process and, wait for it, your name will go on a list.

"Oh no! Not a list!" you say. "The sheriff is going to huff and puff and blow my house down! Then I'm going to jail!"
Nope. Welcome to the injustice system.

Unless you go and get pulled over or arrested for doing something else idiotic, nobody is coming for you. You can carry on with your empty, pathetic existence and, barring any further non-compliance with the law, you're good to go. When push comes to shove, the warrant, like all of the other judgments and court orders, are little more than pieces of paper. Flimsy, unenforceable bullshit.

If, for some strange reason, you do find yourself in the county jail, you don't actually have to pay the sum of money required on the bench warrant because, evidently, that's also only a recommendation. If you can spare a few bucks for your kid that day, chances are, you'll be out in hours, no harm done. Even if you're as broke as you claim, and have no money to fund your release, you're still only going to be held for 72 hours max. You'll probably be out in time to make it to happy hour and the bartender will probably buy you a drink to celebrate. Good grief.

But wait, there's more!

Stubborn wage garnishment got you down? Do I have a solution for you! Quit your high-paying, white-collar job, or get fired, whatever rocks your boat, and get a job in a restaurant When your income is cash-based and mostly unaccounted for, there are no wages to be garnished so you can keep all of your cash and invest it in bitches and booze.

Worried about making that lump sum payment that you've owed for five years? Worry no more, my flaming friend! If you never open a bank account, rent, rather than own your apartment and don't purchase a vehicle, the courts can't do a damn thing! If you have nothing, or at least appear to, nothing can be taken from you. The only potential circumstances that could result in your child support obligation actually being involuntarily collected from you are if you pay your taxes, which you likely don't, or if you win the lottery, which you likely won't. I'm not going to hold my breath for either.

The moral of the story here, is that if you don't want to have to do anything, just don't do anything and nothing can be done.

The rest of us, however, the doers and makers, the movers and shakers, will have to keep doing it all. That's ok, though, we're used to it. I apologize for bursting anyone's bubble who has big dreams of sharing the cost of orthodontia and higher education but, the truth is, we're on our own. You may have a stack of court orders in your house saying otherwise, piles of papers littered with words like obligation, mandatory and order but, at the end of the day all you have is a pyrrhic victory, a pile of papers, empty words and broken promises.

So, while the flaming assholes are breaking your balls and beating the system; failing to meet their parental obligations and financial responsibilities, at least you have a massive fucking stack of papers you can light on fire to keep warm when the electricity is shut off because, unlike the child support department, the electric company doesn't fuck around with the word obligation.

27: On the Rocks

Suggested Pairing: Punch Romaine

If the ship's —a- sinking, we're going down drinking.

1 egg white

1 ounce white wine

1/2 ounce lemon juice

2 ounces Champagne or sparkling wine

Twist of orange peel

1 ounce white rum

1/2 ounce simple syrup

1 ounce fresh orange juice

In an ice-filled cocktail shaker, combine egg white, rum, wine, simple syrup, lemon and orange juice; shake vigorously until well mixed and frothy. Mound crushed ice in a large coupe glass, and pour drink around it. Top with champagne, and garnish with orange peel.

This frothy, fanciful concoction was served at the final first class dinner aboard the Titanic.

Cheers.

My sincerest gratitude to the generous individual who posted a real-time animated recreation of the sinking of the Titanic online several weeks ago. That was just the uplifting, awe-inspiring two hour and forty minute piece of technologically brilliant and mind-blowingly depressing bullshit I needed to keep me company for a significant portion of an already sleepless night.

My initial reaction to watching this video, besides obviously drinking wine and quietly singing "My Heart Will Go On" off-key, was to ponder what kind of asshole has the time and wherewithal to create such a disturbing masterpiece. My second reaction was obviously drinking wine and pondering what kind of asshole I was to sit alone and watch it, in its entirety, in the middle of the night. Neither wine nor Xanax could steal this moment of whatever the opposite of bliss is, and trust and believe, I had my moment. One hundred and sixty of them that night, to be precise.

I don't think I need to explain this video to you in great detail. Sufficed to say, a big fucking ship sunk in the middle of a bigger fucking ocean and, start to finish, it took thirty-five minutes less than it did for poor Rose and Jack. What I will tell you is that, although you might say you won't, you'll probably watch it. You may watch only parts, or you may just watch the beginning and the end, which would be a mystery to me considering we all know what happens in the end, but you are probably already googling it as we speak.

The creator of this picturesque, Pixar-esque film did do us the favor of leaving out the people and all of their horrifying screaming and dying, which ironically made the whole experience rather meditative. It was like the mental patient's version of listening to an ocean sounds cd while downward-dogging. I was one with myself and my wine, and had found a suitable soundtrack for the occasion.

I do think I need to explain to you under what type of fucked up conditions I decided to spend an evening on a virtual sinking ship. Earlier that day, I had the displeasure of reuniting with my ex-husband and my ex-in-laws for a fun-filled dysfunctional family meeting.

I could really end this story right here and it would make perfect sense.

Anyone with exes or in-laws, or God forbid both, just fixed themselves a cocktail and said a silent amen.

My life, the ship deemed unsinkable, collided that day with the in-law iceberg. Despite being an experienced captain and knowing the dangers of those waters, I moved forward, full steam, with ire and indiscretion. I screamed, "Assholes, right ahead!" And we collided in a fury of pent-up resentment and bitterness, but also with the best intentions and highest hopes. It seemed inevitable that we would all end up treading water until the ocean went dark and still. Why, you might be wondering, would I participate in such an act of masochism?

Like those poor fucks doomed to die on the Titanic that night in the middle of the icy North Atlantic, I was, yet again searching for a lifeboat for my son. While his relationship with his father may appear dead in the water, when it comes to a boy and his dad, much like when it comes to Jack and Rose, you never fucking let go. Now I know that fifty percent of you reading this think I'm an asshole for subjecting my son to another round of the Deadbeat Dad Olympics, setting him up for inevitable and inconceivable disappointment.

I also know that the other fifty percent believe I am doing the right thing by giving my son whatever chance he has at a semi-normal father/son experience. I know these things to be true because half of me agrees with me and half of me doesn't. I'm an asshole doing the right thing, is essentially what it boils down to. I am patting myself on the back with one hand and slapping myself across the face with the other.

The first fifty percent of you that thought I was an asshole are, in fact assholes too, because we actually made a marginal amount of progress at that meeting. My son has decided to speak to his father again, which is bigger than you might be inclined to believe, and they saw each other for the first time in almost five months. My little man opened the mailbox on his ninth birthday and there was a card in it, from his dad, the first one he's ever sent.

Now, I'm not deluded enough to believe that life is going to be rainbows and sunshine from here on out, but something's better than nothing, right? I have to believe that there is hope. I can't give up, not yet.

So, I find myself at a crossroads in the water in terms of exit strategy with regard to my ex. Give it another shot or call it a day?

If you're the cute old couple hugging in their bed in their stateroom, you choose a quick but certain death and, just like that, it's all over. But if you're Leonardo DiCaprio, you hold onto the railings and ride that bitch into the depths of the ocean and pray for a miracle.

I choose to be Kate Winslet in this delusion, thank you. She's bold and brave and, best of all, she survives. And she has a British accent which makes mostly everything more tolerable.

If I have learned nothing else from the unthinkable and unsinkable, it is survival. I have taught my son that, no matter what, we will be ok because, while life can be sad and lonely and difficult, it is a beautiful mess that we are fortunate to be a part of.

I always wonder if I'm doing the right thing and maybe I'm not, but that's ok too. We don't always get it right the first time but the point is to keep on trying. Shit, the Titanic sank on its maiden voyage, so I think we're doing pretty well over here, all things being equal.

The simple truth and the silver lining when it comes to sinking ships, literal or figurative, is that nine times out of ten they come equipped with lifeboats. You want to know what else? Women and children get on those lifeboats before anyone else on board is allowed to. So, if the ship we're on is going to sink, I'm going to hang on until we make it to shore. Hopefully his father will eventually find his way, but there is no more room left on our lifeboat.

Shortly before one AM, I stood up that evening after watching the ship go down, and I envisioned the ensemble playing their final song as the waters rushed aboard. Even in tragedy there is beauty and, it was with that thought, that I saluted the Titanic, and myself for being so committed to watching it sink, and I went to bed. I slept well that night.

28: Beer Muscles

Suggested pairing: Liquid Courage

Don't be a pussy.

1 pint milk

4-6 scoops of ice cream

8-12 ounces Crème de Cacao

6 ounces vodka

6 ounces white rum

Combine all ingredients in a blender and liquefy until shake-like consistency. Serve in daiquiri glasses.

Cheers.

There is a long list of bullshit that I can blame on my ex-husband. I feel entitled to blame him for a significant portion of my financial woes, home foreclosure and subsequent bankruptcy. I feel justified in faulting him for my son's bouts with anger, resentment and rage as well as his need to fill a fatherly void with action figures and Nerf guns.

I believe that he maintains a noteworthy level of culpability with regard to my longstanding trust issues and propensity to overanalyze and be suspicious. He has continued for years and years to cram his dirty laundry into my already overstuffed baggage, forcing me to bear the weighty burden of his behavior for both of us.

While I maintain my right to be royally pissed off at him for all of this and more, there is one underlying issue I just can't pin on him because, I admit, it is mine, all mine – and that is anxiety.

I have been anxious for as long as I can obsessively recall. As a young girl, I was a super shy nail-biter who was incapable of surviving a sleepover outside of my own home. I struggled to play in groups, was unpopular at school and had to be picked up by my parents on the first night of Girl Scout Camp.

As I matured, my nervousness and introversion spiraled into full blown OCD and generalized anxiety. I checked locks and counted in my head and obsessed about death and dying. Eventually, or inevitably, the anxiety became less generalized and more centered around sheer panic. In my first period English class in 8th grade, upon distribution of a vocabulary quiz, I experienced my first onset of migraine symptoms. Of course, my teacher thought I was a lying little shit and hadn't studied, but I couldn't read, or even see, the entire right side of the page.

Shit just got better and better from there.

Enter the dreaded panic attack. I'm not sure if you've ever had the utter displeasure of experiencing this, and I'm so sorry if you have, but a panic attack exists somewhere in the vicinity of childbirth and kidney stones. I know because I drew the proverbial short stick or pillaged a village in a past life, and have had the indescribable joy of all three. Childbirth is awful, but you get a child out of the deal, so I guess it's a tradeoff. Kidney stones blow hard because it's similar on the pain scale to labor, only you don't get to name and cradle your rough, pebble-like bundle of joy when you produce it. You can, however, take it home in a jar. I did. I earned it.

A panic attack, though, holy shit. Beyond the obvious psychological terror and physical trauma, it's just bizarre and illogical and uncalled for. A panic attack, at least for me, usually begins with an already irrational thought process and devolves from there into sweating, shaking, crying and hyperventilation. It lasts somewhere between fifteen minutes and an hour, depending upon when I decide to change my environment, and is untamed by reason, comfort or support. It just eventually passes. It's an emotional fucking kidney stone, now that I think about it.

Now, you may be reading this and thinking to yourself that I am a total fucking nut, and you may be right, but at least I'm honest about it. We all have our crosses to bear and, while this may be a major life issue, I sleep well at night knowing I'm a loony but decent human being. Especially after taking a Xanax.

I'd like to say that as I have grown and gained wisdom and experience, that my anxiety has lessened but, the truth is, it's just evolved. I have managed to elude the panic attacks for the majority of the last year and my OCD is totally in check. Except for checking to make sure the burners on the stove are off and the gate to the backyard is secured, and I like to think of those as just the safety measures of a slightly crazy person.

Unfortunately, as this disorder has shifted away from obsession, compulsion and panic, it has affected an aspect of my life that really needed no more fucking with at this particular juncture, and that is my ability to socialize like a normal human being.

Here's the deal. I look forward to my drive home alone from work each day, listening to the radio, smoking a cigarette and basking in unadulterated, un-children-infested peace. One would think that I would spend these fleeting moments with a smile on my face, the wind in my hair and a Zen-like Om whirling about my head. But, alas, this is when my brain goes on a bender.

I exhibit the typical worries of a single working mother. Is my son going to be ok? Am I doing a good job? How am I ever going to pay for this shit? Totally average, every day concerns for a parent, but it doesn't end there. I often allow my mind to wander to dark, dangerous places and overextend its stay. I have wasted millions of moments of my life rehashing conversations, wondering what I may have said that could have possibly offended somebody. I have the unsubstantiated yet unyielding fear that I could be terminated from my job at any given moment because of some major fuck up that I can't be sure I committed. I worry, and obsess, and panic for no reason whatsoever, except that that's what I do.

Lately, as what I believe to be a result of my own deep-seated, ingrained thoughts and fears in conjunction with the sad state of affairs we are in as a world, my anxiety has shifted into the safety zone.

My fearful fire is being fueled by news broadcasts and lockdown drills and widespread panic. I wonder and worry about the man walking alone on the sidewalk across the street from my son's school at drop-off in the morning, and wait for him to be a safe distance away prior to exiting the parking lot. I spend the entirety of the coming attractions portion of an animated movie-going experience surveying the audience, questioning why some don't have popcorn or entered or exited at what I deem to be suspicious times.

This hyper-sensitivity peaked last month when I purchased concert tickets and, at the last minute, declined to attend. The tickets were to see my favorite band. With my favorite people. At my favorite venue.

I can't believe I backed out, but I did. Out of fear. Out of anxiety.

The concert was not just an awesome show, with close friends at a kick-ass location.

It was the Indigo Girls. Playing at the Stone Pony. During Pride. A week after the Orlando massacre.

I could not do it.

I am a live music junkie – it's what I love and what I live for, but all I could think about in the days before the show was how we would get out if we needed to. The entrance, the bathroom, the floor packed wall to wall with people. I felt suffocated, like the walls of the club were preemptively closing in around me. I felt frightened that some fucking nut-job might walk in, guns blazing and take us all out in the midst of a rousing rendition of "Tangled Up in Blue."
Most of all, though, I felt ashamed.

I felt ashamed that my fear got in the way of my fun. I felt ashamed that I was unable to overcome my own issues long enough to enjoy an evening out with friends. I felt ashamed that I had begun to assume the worst of all people because of the actions of a few.
I could sit here and say that my actions, or inactions that evening were the result of other people's hatred and violence, but the truth is that the only person responsible for what I do is me.

The same wisdom can be applied to all the shit that my ex has done, and continues to blame me for. When we divorced, we divided assets and issues – I left with my own credit card debt, the dining room table, sole custody and my generalized anxiety; he with his Jeep Wrangler, 401K and his alcoholism. While he and his family claim that he drinks because I know how to push his buttons, I know that, while he does add an extra level of fucked up to my already nervous disposition, I do this to myself. He may have hit a few out of the ballpark when my bases were already loaded but I'm the one that put three runners on before he ever came to bat.

I can't continue to allow myself to be controlled by what has happened in the past or what may happen in the future. I won't continue to be afraid of the what ifs and the what the fucks.

I will not be deterred from sharing my experiences because I am afraid of what people might think or what might happen to me if I do.

There's a good chance that a certain someone may see fit to sue me for writing this. Fuck it, I'm doing it anyway. Obviously. The silver lining of that particular lawsuit will be that if there is money awarded to him because he got a booboo on his feelings since I spoke the truth, those funds will be deferred immediately into my child support account to pay for all the shit he couldn't pay for while he was paying for a lawyer.

I'm not afraid anymore.
Check out my beer muscles.

29: Last Call

Suggested pairing: The Jersey Turnpike

Last call for alcohol, last exit before Crazytown.

Ingredients:

Leftover alcohol

Bar mats

Shot glass

Balls of steel

Wring all remaining alcohol spilled on to bar mats into a shot glass in no particular order and with no regard for human life, whatsoever. Do not chill. Do not strain. Do not care.

Cheers.

One can go to Bartending School to learn the trade or one can learn from experience. I chose the latter and, in the process, I learned a wealth of information about alcohol and the individuals who consume it. My repertoire ranges from menial tasks like operating a POS system, stocking shelves and filling ice bins to more refined skills like getting people to like you enough to buy you shots and tip you, pouring the exact amount of a half dozen ingredients into a shaker and filling a shot glass to the brim without waste, and being able to zero out a register and count tips while wasted.

Bartending is no simple feat, certainly not one I would reattempt at this stage in my life. It is managing the quintessential special education classroom, the only difference being that your students are adults, moronic ones mostly, and socially lubricated with booze. Thanks very much, but I'll stick with teaching tweens that think IDK is not only a word, but not at all an inappropriate response to a test question.

The greatest gift of knowledge that was ever bestowed upon me as a bartender was the Jersey Turnpike shot. It is the gift that keeps on giving, and the joy it brings lives on forever behind the bar inside my mind.

The Jersey Turnpike is exactly what you would expect an adult beverage to be if you are one of those assholes that constantly remarks on how disgusting of a place New Jersey is to live, likely having never traversed beyond, well, the Jersey Turnpike. What exit? Shut the fuck up. Newsflash: most of us don't live directly off of the Turnpike or the Parkway and have no fucking clue what exits you are referring to.

The Garden State is fucking beautiful. We have shitloads of acres of preserved farmland, gorgeous turn-of-the-century buildings and quaint little towns that would leave your big-ass mouth speechless. Yes, the turnpike is gross. There are as many smokestacks as there are potholes and you may think that we drive like assholes when, in fact, we just know how to navigate the road, and probably life, better than most.

In any event, I learned how to make this divine creation at the tail end of a long shift behind the bar, when the remaining customers were a few regulars that had put in a full day dancing on my last nerve, and a group of douchebag frat boys celebrating their buddy's 21st birthday in the expected sleeveless, penniless, classless fashion. Sure boys, I'll get you another round of red-headed sluts, and I'll be back promptly to wipe your vomit and whatever remaining dignity from the bar.

Needless to say, I was done with these fuckers, and you would be too if your job was to wait on idiots for hours as they become increasingly intoxicated and intolerable. As the night wound down and the boys wound up, the clock ticked dangerously and gloriously close to last call, and it was then that the alcohol angels shined down upon me. The boys ordered one final round of shots for their boy and uttered the phrase that made it all possible and, frankly, made life worth living at that moment.
"Surprise us."

As my eyes nearly rolled back into my skull and across the filthy bar floor, my co-worker nodded to me and, with a delightfully mischievous grin, let me know that it was all under control. My job was to just sit back and enjoy.

And I did.

The young men paid no mind to the fact that the other bartender was gracefully making her way about the bar, wringing out the bar mats and rags into a pint glass, one that slowly rose in volume and disgustingness until it brimmed with muck and all my heart's desires. I can't begin to explain what could have been, and must have been residing in that glass but I'm certain it was teeming with bacteria and bottom shelf booze. She then strained the concoction into shot glasses and served them to our poor and unsuspecting clients, who hastily raised their glasses with one final cheers to the birthday boy, going down the hatch and down the Turnpike.
Bliss in its purest form.

What's so striking about a moment like this is that we all got to experience our own version of happiness. The boys, drunk and rowdy, were just thrilled to be drunk and rowdy, and to have two decent looking bartenders slinging shots for them. The bartenders, tired and punchy, were ecstatic to perform a bar trick, necessitating absolutely no sleight of hand, yet resulting in Houdini like glee on our side of the bar. All was right with the world.

Don't get me wrong, this was fucking wrong. But it felt so right. Even when you combine the worst of the worst, creating something that is even worser, as my fine English students would say, there can be something good that comes out of it in the end, believe it or not.

If you look at life as though it were just a local pub existing somewhere in the universe, ironically, everything begins to make sense. The vast majority of customers are good people, and just want to connect and have fun with other good people. They want to make friends, sing songs, dance a little and have cocktails with others out to do the same. These people respect others' boundaries, follow the rules and pay for their shit.

Then there are the assholes.

The people who want to split a $14 tab onto three credit cards. The people who leave change as a tip. Those who snap their fingers, call you baby and drink Bud Light from a can. These are the individuals who will walk out on their checks, fall asleep at the bar or act like they own the place because they "know somebody." But, as bartenders, it is not our position to engage with these assholes. That is why we have bouncers, and karma and the mob.

We encounter these people every day in life: the good, the bad and the ugly, but it is not our job to change them or to make them better. It is our job, like the bartender, to smile, go about our business and keep it moving knowing that we will never resort to being an asshole of that caliber.

I have learned through my vast and unwanted experience with my ex-husband that you can't argue with crazy, you can't expect an old dog to learn new tricks, and close only counts in horseshoes and hand grenades. Actually, I learned that last one from my dad.
What will my son learn from his dad?

He will learn the importance of not being an asshole.
What will my son learn from me?
Everything else.

He has already learned sarcasm and a shit-ton of curse words from me so I'd like to think my work here is done. But there are other things I have, and will teach him that are almost as important as the versatile functions of the word fuck. I will teach him to have pride in himself whether he is an athlete, a scholar, a bartender, a writer, gay, straight, confident or anxious. I will teach him that there is always a way. It may be a rough road or a windy path but, whether you have to jump through hoops to reach your goal or scale mountains, there is always a way. There is ALWAYS a way. I will teach him to respect himself and women and everyone who is different because that is what is right and what is holy. I will teach him that he can be anything he wants in this world and he can, and will be better than me, and certainly his father.

I will teach my son to persevere.
I will teach him to always tip the bartender.

Life can be a big bag of burning shit at times, but it's not about the bag of shit we're handed, rather what we make of it. My sweet son, despite his father's lack of participation and all around douchebaggery, is phenomenal. He is genuine and hysterical and resilient. He is, as I sit writing this, outside my window fencing with himself. For the first time in his life, he has found a passion for something, not to fulfil a need to fit in or because it was forced upon him, not because his dad said he should or because I want to live vicariously through him, but because he enjoys it.

This is a testament to him as an individual and to me as a mother, and it feels like the sweetest moment in the history of the universe. Not only is he fencing, but he is functioning, excelling. And he is doing so all on his own, without the presence of a father.

It may not be easy, but everything is going to be ok.

The Jersey Turnpike is a foul, nasty beverage comprised of shit you would never, ever want to put in your mouth under any circumstance and, yet, given the right scenario can bring pleasure to the one drinking it.

The night that I served my first Jersey Turnpike shot was just like any other night behind the bar. It ended the same way every other night behind that bar ended. The lights went up. We did the last call. The music died down. And the manager said what he always said, and what will forever be true.

You don't have to go home, but you can't stay here.
I refuse to stay here any longer.